USA *Today* Bestseller
Los Angeles Times Bestseller
Wall Street Journal Bestseller

"Ryan is not only charming and hilarious, he could sell milk to a cow. This book is going to be very helpful and humorous to a lot of people looking to up their business game."
—Andy Cohen, host of *Watch What Happens Live*...and *New York Times* bestselling author of *Superficial*

"*Sell It Like Serhant* cuts to the heart of what it takes to build a great sales career—passion, curiosity, and being willing to do almost anything."
—Larry King, host of *Larry King Now* and *New York Times* bestselling author of *My Remarkable Journey*

"Sales are the foundation of any company, and this must-read book shows you how to master it. Ryan's journey as he sharpened his own sales skills is truly inspiring and something every salesperson or entrepreneur needs to learn from."
—Daymond John, star of ABC's *Shark Tank* and *New York Times* bestselling author of *Rise and Grind*

"Selling—your product, your service, even yourself—has changed more in the past 10 years than in the previous 100. That's why you need this book. Drawing on his incredible success selling real estate in one of the world's most pressure-cooker markets, Ryan Serhant offers smart, practical, modern guidance for getting, keeping, and serving customers and clients. Whatever you do for a living, you'll do it better if you learn to sell like Serhant."
—Daniel Pink, *New York Times* bestselling author of *When* and *To Sell is Human*

"Ryan Serhant is the authority on all things selling. If you want to sell more than anyone else, read this now."

—Gary Vaynerchuk, *New York Times* bestselling author of *Crushing It!: How Great Entrepreneurs Build Their Business and Influence—and How You Can, Too*

"Whether you're in real estate or an author, you have to know how to sell yourself and your work. Because if you don't, you can't eat. This book from one of America's hardest hustling salesmen is a crash course into becoming great at it."

—Ryan Holiday, bestselling author of *The Obstacle Is the Way* and *Ego Is the Enemy*

"*Sell It Like Serhant* is the only sales book you'll ever need. Ryan Serhant distills the secrets to achieving long term sales success for making more money and gaining freedom in your life. Ryan's sales methodology and techniques can benefit anyone regardless of industry, profession, and income level. Whether you're just starting out, or looking to up your game, this is the book for you."

—Dan Schawbel, *New York Times* and *Wall Street Journal* bestselling author of *Promote Yourself* and *Back to Human*

"This book isn't just about sales, it's about self-improvement overall. If you're looking to maximize your potential, you should read Ryan's book."

—Lewis Howes, *New York Times* bestselling author of *The School of Greatness*

"You want a big life on your own terms, and *Sell It Like Serhant* provides excellent advice that will help you boost your confidence, expand your network and sell yourself or your ideas to absolutely anyone."

—Ann Shoket, former editor-in-chief at
Seventeen Magazine and author of *The Big Life*

"Full of smart tricks and tips to make a seller out of you."

—PEOPLE.com

SELL IT LIKE SERHANT

HOW TO SELL MORE, EARN MORE, AND BECOME THE ULTIMATE SALES MACHINE

RYAN SERHANT

hachette
BOOKS

NEW YORK BOSTON

Copyright © 2019 by Ryan Serhant
Cover design by Amanda Kain
Cover photographs by Heidi Gutman-Guillaume
Cover copyright © 2019 by Hachette Book Group, Inc.

Hachette Book Group supports the right to free expression and the value of copyright. The purpose of copyright is to encourage writers and artists to produce the creative works that enrich our culture.

The scanning, uploading, and distribution of this book without permission is a theft of the author's intellectual property. If you would like permission to use material from the book (other than for review purposes), please contact permissions@hbgusa.com. Thank you for your support of the author's rights.

Hachette Books
Hachette Book Group
1290 Avenue of the Americas, New York, NY 10104
hachettebooks.com
twitter.com/hachettebooks

First Paperback Edition: September 2019

Hachette Books is a division of Hachette Book Group, Inc. The Hachette Books name and logo are trademarks of Hachette Book Group, Inc.

The publisher is not responsible for websites (or their content) that are not owned by the publisher.

The Hachette Speakers Bureau provides a wide range of authors for speaking events. To find out more, go to www.hachettespeakersbureau.com or call (866) 376-6591.

Graphics credit to Kristen Kipilla

Library of Congress Control Number: 2018938760

ISBNs: 978-0-31644-957-1 (hardcover), 978-0-31644-956-4 (ebook), 978-1-54911-603-2 (audio downloadable), 978-1-54911-663-6 (audio CD); 978-0-31644-958-8 (paperback)

Printed in the United States of America

LSC-C

10   9   8   7   6   5   4   3

This book is dedicated to my wife Emilia, for believing in me from day one. You push me to do more than I ever imagined possible and inspire me to reach higher every day.

And to my Dad, who instilled in me a #ReadySetGO mind-set, and taught me that while there are a lot of things in life that you can't control, how hard you work isn't one of them.

Author's Note

I've changed some of the names and identifying details throughout this book. I'd also like to add that while I can remember the
exact address of every apartment I've ever sold and when I sold
it, I can't say that I remember all the conversations I've had with
people with the same freaky level of accuracy. I've attempted to
recapture conversations to the extent that my memory allows.

Contents

Introduction

I started my sales career on Monday, September 15, 2008. Do you remember that day? That was also the day Lehman Brothers filed for the largest bankruptcy in history, collapsing the subprime mortgage industry and setting the stage for what we now call the Great Recession. Imagine how hard it was for a new salesperson like me—one who lacked confidence, didn't own a suit, and had no idea how to go about making a sale—to sell real estate at that time. As you can imagine, I didn't get off to a great start. In 2009, I made just over $9,000. In 2017, nine years later, I turned 33, and had done 472 deals, equaling nearly one billion dollars in sales. During a global financial crisis, in one of the toughest markets in the country, *a salesman was born.*

On *Million Dollar Listing New York*, I am the very confident guy who wears nice suits, traverses the island of Manhattan with a driver, and closes $2–$3 million in sales every day. On my reality show *Sell It Like Serhant*, I use my sales expertise to transform salespeople who are struggling to sell everything from golf balls to hot tubs into selling machines. But growing up I was the opposite of the guy you see on TV. My family moved a lot. I was overweight, painfully shy, and socially awkward. I tried every sport ever invented and sucked at every one. Put a ball directly in my hand and I'd drop it. Toss me one thousand balls and I'd miss every single one. I had zero confidence and was scared of everything. I was so emotional that I earned the nickname "Cryin' Ryan." I felt most comfortable with the theatre kids, where it was okay to wear ridiculous costumes and pretend to be someone you weren't. I was the kid home alone on Friday nights eating Jell-O pudding and watching Nickelodeon in a ruffled blouse.

I went through an awkward Shakespeare phase as a kid that led to studying theatre in college. After graduation, I moved to New York City to be an actor. Me and about a billion other people!

It was only a few years ago that I was an unemployed thespian struggling to make rent in New York City. My dream of being a famous actor was getting crushed along with my self-worth. I made some money here and there from work as a hand model, but it was never enough to cover even the most basic expenses. My credit card was declined at the grocery store, and I'd hand out flyers on the street to get people to sign up for a local gym in exchange for free workouts. Being broke is an awful position to be in, especially in New York City, and I had to find a way to make money unless I wanted to move back home with my parents. It was my first time living on my own and I wanted to make it work. I could have been the clichéd actor-waiter. But who wants to miss an audition because of a shift at TGI Fridays? Instead, I got my real estate license so I could work whenever I wanted and my schedule would be my own. I would learn how to rent apartments to people, and do a deal or two each month so I could cover my bills.

When I first started, I was a mess. I couldn't sell a thing. Other brokers I worked with were constantly closing deals, and I used to kill myself wondering, How are they doing this? And how can I do it? I was tireless, I tried different tactics, and, eventually, after years of hard work, I discovered a secret that gave me a huge advantage: *I had the most balls in the air.* I was never hyper-focused on one ball. I didn't put all my energy into one sale or one client. I'd go from a closing with one client straight to a showing with another client, and took calls for offers while in the taxi. I didn't live or die by one deal. I never closed a sale and wondered, "What now?" because the next deal was already happening. My *more balls up* approach gave me a big edge, and I quickly became a top seller.

Think back to when you were a little kid and the bulk of your day mainly involved playing with toys. You'd be happily building a Lego tower, then think, "I'm over this. I want to play with my racecar set *now.*" But Mom says you should put one toy away before getting out another. If you don't do it, she'll freak out about the big mess you've created. *You have no discipline! There's no order!* We all know kids don't want to put away their toys. Why would they do that when they can be completely surrounded by cool, fun things, moving effortlessly from one toy to the next? I will admit to being fairly OCD. I enjoy a clean, neat environment. But the message we are given as children, that one thing must be put perfectly back in order before we *even think* about touching something else, is bad advice. What's wrong with playing with all of the toys while keeping them easily accessible? As we get older, this message of "only one thing at a time" has been ingrained in our brains—and we go into the business world thinking the same way. We handle one client before moving on to the next. We close one deal before we focus on another. We treat our clients and deals like objects that need to be carefully tucked away on a shelf before we take on more. My sales theory is not about putting your clients away—it's about how to keep them out in front of you, accessible, so that you can manage everything appropriately and yield the same great results. That kid who has learned to organize her toys just right, so she can move from one thing to the next with ease? That kid is a great salesperson in the making. She's got the right mind-set, and I call that mind-set Balls Up.

More balls* up means you're surrounded by opportunity and you're taking advantage of those opportunities at the same time—you're making news contacts, gaining great referrals, and maximizing the hours you're awake. Despite what we're taught as kids and in sales, to manage one deal at a time, I discovered that it takes just as much time and energy to manage one deal as it does six. Some balls are quick—and can be dealt with right

---

* You may have noticed by now that I have used the word "balls" several times, even in these first few pages—I just want to say that, yes, I know balls are also testicles. If that's where your mind goes every time I say "balls" in this book—well, then, laugh your way through this book!

away. Sometimes if you toss a ball up high, that gives you time to handle a few other balls before it drops back down to you. I learned that it is possible to control their flight path—meaning, it's possible to manage many balls successfully. So, why grab just one ball when you can handle five or more? Go big.

Anyone can get lucky and accomplish one huge sale. You sold a $30,000 grand piano or a six-figure rug? That's awesome. But can you do it again tomorrow? What about the day after that? Did you sell anything else? If you want to have a successful sales track record, you must understand that sales is a volume business. It's that simple. If you want to make it, you have to sell more of your product than anyone else. It's not about one sale; it's about every sale you make. Being the ultimate sales machine isn't as simple as following a bunch of tricks and tips. Anyone can do that. Sometimes to become good salespeople, we must strip apart our old ideas and build ourselves back up into a more productive and more awesome version of who we are. It's about relearning what it means to be a salesperson. You already have what it takes to succeed, and this book is going to help you be more productive and reach your full potential.

People ask me all the time, "How did you do it? How can I sell as much as you?" This is always crazy for me to hear, because not long ago; I was the one asking these exact same questions. I know what it feels like to be a salesperson who isn't hitting his mark. In 2009, I wasn't well connected and I hadn't sold anything since I was eight years old, when my brother and I would sell firewood to our neighbors. How was I going to build a sales career from scratch? In this book, I'm going to share stories behind some of my craziest deals and show you how I created a sales career from nothing and then kept going. This book isn't my life story—seriously. I'm only 33. And it's not a memoir about selling real estate in New York City (snore). In *Sell It Like Serhant*, I'm sharing all of my trade secrets. What you are reading is essentially my playbook about how to sell absolutely anything at all.

You'll learn how to structure your day to maximize time and keep balls in the air. I'll teach you the art of follow-up and share sales techniques that I've developed over the course of my career—the strategies that have made my team one of the top sales teams in the entire country. And also, you'll learn how to enjoy selling. Selling *is fun*—no matter what you sell. And a lot of stuff is being sold everywhere. EVERY. SINGLE. DAY. You might as well be the one selling too. After all, if kid Ryan who couldn't walk down the hall at school without being bullied can now sell $60 million every month (actually $101,861,229 last month, but who's counting?) in one of the most competitive markets in the world, then anyone can. Let's get you to the next level together. Deal?

Ready, set, GO!

CHAPTER 1

The Birth of a Salesman

New York is actually a fairly easy city to navigate. Most of the streets are laid out in a nice, neat, orderly grid. If I drop off my 92-year-old grandmother from Wisconsin in the middle of Times Square, Nana could find her way around with no problem. Downtown Manhattan, anything below 14th Street, is a totally different story. Sure, the West Village is quaint, with cobblestones, quiet streets, and Federal-style townhouses. But the street layout can make about as much sense as a four-year-old trying to solve algebra problems. It's weird and confusing. This should explain why one of my first clients, Jessica, was so annoyed with me. Jessica was a twenty-something who responded to my ad on Craigslist. That's how new brokers like me found clients in 2008. We placed ads, clients called, and we arranged to meet with them. It's actually very similar to arranging a date with a prostitute.

Jessica had a budget of $2,500 a month. She wanted a two-bedroom she could convert into three bedrooms, so she and her two roommates (who were also both named Jessica, by the way) could fit. I was taking her to an apartment on Morton Street that might be a good fit for her *and* her mother. Her mother was her guarantor. Meaning, she was responsible for paying the rent if Jessica and the other Jessicas lost their jobs or spent all of their money on designer handbags. Jessica One kept handing me her phone, because her mom, who was in Michigan, insisted I give her a sportscaster's play-by-play of the apartment search.

We had been wandering around for 20 minutes, which is about a decade in New York City time, where everything *must* move quickly. I knew we were really close by, but I couldn't find the right street. You can be lost in the Village even when you know exactly where you are. We were on the corner of Christopher Street and Seventh Avenue, but I didn't know which way Morton Street was. I couldn't afford a Palm Treo or a Black-Berry, the smartphones of the day. The iPhone had just made its debut, but most people didn't have one back then. Every morning I would print out tiny maps and directions for each of my appointments. I'd fold them up in my pocket so I could refer to them if I needed to. Walking with Jessica, I kept trying to sneak a peek at my map, but I couldn't get a good look without her noticing. I tried to sidetrack her by saying that I was giving her a "quick tour of the area." I pointed out the apartment where NBC's sitcom *Friends* was filmed and told her Morton Street was just a couple of blocks away. Ten minutes later it became clear we had circled the block again when we ended up in front of the same newsstand. Between the Mentos and the extensive Snapple selection were newspaper headlines screaming shock words like "PLUNGE!" "CRISIS!" due to a crashing financial market. I was about to face my own mini-crisis with Jessica.

She had had it. She glared at me, like she was whipping me the finger with her eyes. "Oh my God. What is *wrong* with you?!"

she shouted. "You shouldn't be allowed to show apartments to humans. Ever." She stuck out her arm and a taxi screeched to a stop in front of her. She jumped in and sped off, leaving me standing on the street in my cowboy boots feeling pathetic and lame.

What if she was right? I glanced back at the newsstand. The headlines were taunting me. There was a terrible recession. Why was I trying to sell real estate when the economy had fallen to pieces? I was nearly out of money. I felt almost destined to be one of those guys in his parents' basement playing video games in his underwear and eating Yodels.

Enter Ben Kennedy.

I headed back to the office uptown on 49th and Madison, thinking I couldn't feel any worse. It turned out I could feel way worse, thanks to my arch nemesis Ben Kennedy. Ben was from the Midwest and barely said a word to anyone around the office, other than the occasional restrained hello. But Ben was a great broker. As I dragged myself back to my desk I could hear Ben closing another deal—probably his tenth rental deal of the day. While he was bringing in piles of signed leases and earning huge commission checks, I was roaming around the city lost. How did he do it? I had a top-notch education, came from a good family, and was a preppy-looking actor with a gleaming smile! What does he have that I don't? He barely even speaks! My ego couldn't understand it. How was he constantly closing deals when I couldn't rent a single convertible three-bedroom walk-up to Jessica-to-the-third-power?

I had reached a low point, and I needed to talk to someone. I decided to call my older brother Jimmy. He was 10 years older than me and had what I deemed a real life. He had a wife and kids, and a solid job in finance. Jimmy has always looked out for me. He helped me move to New York City, he was with me when I opened my first bank account, and he showed me how to get a credit card. Surely he could crack the mystery of why Ben Kennedy was killing it and I was broke. I crawled out onto the fire escape with my flip phone and scrolled down to Jimmy's office number. Before he could even say hello, I was on a major rant about quitting, sucking, life sucking, Ben Kennedy sucking, and I-work-soooo-hard. I continued with my sob story even with other phones ringing in the background of Jimmy's office along with the sounds of people doing important things like making money and succeeding at life. My brother was clearly busy, and before I could spit out the words "I've had it! I'm quitt…," he cut me off with:

"Stop being such a little bitch. You've been working as a real estate agent for five minutes. Suck it up. If Ben Kennedy can do it, you can too."

Click. "Hello? Jimmy?"

Oh my God, did he hang up??

Oh. He did.

I crawled back in the window just as Ben Kennedy was getting off the phone. He leaned back in his chair with the most satisfied smile on his face—like he had just rented out an entire apartment building, or maybe the Empire State Building. I walked straight over to Ben Kennedy's desk. Before I got too nervous, I blurted out, "Hey, Ben, so? Um, how do you rent so many apartments? What do you do? I'm new to this and trying to figure it all out and you're awesome, so it would be great to get a few tips from the best in the biz! Buddy!"

Ben looked me up and down—taking in my cowboy boots, the khakis, and my belt with the oversized and jarringly shiny buckle (this was my nice outfit, by the way)—and said, "Nah, man. I ain't tellin' you shit." It was the most I ever heard him say.

TURNING POINT, TAKE ONE

There's no doubt that transforming yourself into a selling machine like the Terminator—but without the violent killings—won't happen overnight. You will have periods in your career when there are more questions than answers. You won't know how to close every deal, handle every client's issue, or have all the answers for your team. But just take a step, even if it's small, and you'll be closer to it. Don't doubt the magnitude that a small action can ultimately have. No one will hand you a secret formula for success. You will realize what the formula is only after you've created it.

Serhant Secret #1

The secret to your success will be revealed in hindsight.
You won't recognize it until you've already lived it.

Ben Kennedy wasn't telling me shit. Okay, fine. My reaction could have been, "Ben is such a dick. People suck!" I could have decided at that moment to quit real estate. I could have begged my mother to buy me a plane ticket home and left New York City forever. Who needs Manhattan when you could move back home and your parents have all the cable channels and the kitchen is stocked with Oreos and ice cream—my two favorite foods, next to Twizzlers, Lucky Charms, and chicken fettuccini alfredo. But my brother's insult was running through my head on repeat. Was I really working as hard as I thought? I wouldn't say a light-bulb went off but there was a mild flicker, and the light was just bright enough for me to see that, hmm, maybe Jimmy was right. Maybe I *was* a little bitch. I had to stop and think. Is this who I want to be? I share a bathroom with 25 people in my apartment building in Koreatown. At night, I stand on a stage located in a basement with my arms up, repeating the line "tick-tock" for 30 consecutive minutes because I've been cast as a clock in a play about Edgar Allan Poe. You know who wasn't playing a clock in a shitty play? Ben Kennedy, that's who. Was this my life? And, more importantly, was it the one I wanted?

For the first time, I really started to think about what I wanted my life to look like. Did I want to drive used cars, wear Gap khakis, take an occasional Caribbean cruise, and eat at Outback Steak-house every Friday? That's a perfectly nice existence. Gap khakis are comfortable, and who wouldn't want to end their week with a plate of Kookaburra Wings and a Melbourne Porterhouse? Or did I want something different? Did I want a life that was completely unhindered by anything? Limitless possibilities. Expansion in all ways. That sounded a lot better than my current situation of broke and in tears. I understood that I had a choice to make. Did I want to be moderately successful? Or did I want to be phenomenally successful? Was I going to be a good broker or the best broker?

I looked over at Ben Kennedy. He was on the phone, chuckling merrily with a client. Maybe I did suck as a salesperson, right now. But was there any reason I couldn't change that?

It didn't matter what made Ben Kennedy so awesome at his job. I didn't need to know the secret to his success. Even if he had leaned over and said, "Okay, Serhant. Here's how I do it: I only eat orange foods and I dance naked under the full moon because I'm also a witch." How would that have helped me? Ben Kennedy had found the secret to his success. It was time for me to find my own. I didn't know how to be a great broker (or even one that just wasn't terrible), but it was time for me to take initiative. I had no idea what my first step would be, but I knew I wanted to take one.

I never planned on being a salesperson. There was no "aha!" moment* for me. The day my brother called me out for my terrible attitude and ridiculous expectation that renting apartments would be as easy as selling Girl Scout cookies was a turning point. It was a small, but significant moment that I could only see in retrospect. My turning point could easily have been missed. It's not as if I got hit by a bus and thought, "Wow. I've come out of this coma against ALL ODDS. I should probably do something amazing with the rest of my life." Don't wait for a dramatic moment to make a move, because it might not come—ever. If you've been planning to be awesome your entire life, now is the time to put a plan into action. Why wait a second longer? Be awesome NOW.

---

* I didn't have an "aha!" moment to launch my career, but while performing Shakespeare in a "park"—a grassy knoll off the West Side Highway— in the middle of NYC traffic alongside a 75-year-old man playing Father Capulet who believed this was his Big Break, I will never forget thinking, *I do not want this to be my future.* I was just happy with each performance that did not end with us all getting run over by a car.

INITIATIVE IS MY FAVORITE WORD

It was time for me to make a serious change, but I had no idea what my first steps would be. I went to bed a low-paid hand model in the most expensive city in the world, and woke up the next day as a real estate broker. And guess what? Both of those guys were totally broke. I had no salary, no benefits, and no handbook on how to succeed at the job. I did not magically transform overnight into someone with contacts, money, sales skills, or even good shoes. But there was one difference: I was excited about going to the office. Going to the office used to be a drag, like a punishment I had to endure until some famous director agreed with me that I should be the next Brad Pitt. I'd stop in between apartment showings to check my voice mail: "You have zero messages," and drink a chai latte at Starbucks until it was time to show another. But the day after the Jimmy-calls-Ryan-a-bitch incident, going to the office felt like a positive. The office felt like an anchor. I stood taller and my shoulders felt lighter. I sat at my desk in the little office above Burger Heaven, and I couldn't imagine how I would get from point A (selling nothing) to point B (selling everything), but I understood that it would take a lot of hard work and initiative. But wait a minute—it turns out that taking initiative was something I definitely understood.

I'd been all about initiative since I arrived in New York City with nothing but a pair of cowboy boots and a bottle of brown hair dye (I started going grey when I was 16). I shared my very first apartment with two roommates from Hamilton College. They were both paralegals, looking to go to law school, who landed jobs with good law firms—the kind that have about fifty names and require insane work hours. I was pursuing my dream of being an actor. I had no boss. I didn't have the same intense schedule or pressures that my roommates had. But my dad, who has always valued hard work and discipline, reminded me that if I wanted to succeed I should work harder than my pre-law, Advil-popping, overcaffeinated roommates. I should get up before they did, work later, and dedicate myself fully to the art of acting. It was good advice. There are a lot of actors in New York City. I'm guessing the number of wannabe actors in NYC is about equal to the city's massive rat population. It's not something you really notice, but if you stop and take a look around you suddenly see they are everywhere. I had to do something. I couldn't just pop into a bodega for a block of tofu and hope the lady in front of me with the giant bag of cat food was actually a casting director and I'd be discovered for the role of "first guy killed" in *Saw XXIII*. I had to take initiative to reach that kind of success.

I realized that taking initiative with my acting career led me to some very unexpected places. I got to play an evil biochemist on a soap opera, I got to run over a guy with a car in an indie film, I was in a production of *Romeo and Juliet* staged along the West Side Highway, and how many people can say they were a hand model? My hands were painted like teapots and dragons to sell phone plans. My hands were all over the world. I was hand famous. Sure, my acting career might not have been the big victory I imagined it would be. It turns out I'm not Brad Pitt. My success as an actor was never even on par with lesser members of the Baldwin or Culkin dynasties. The closest I ever got to feeling like a famous actor was when I told a bouncer at a club I was Dr. Evan Walsh IV from the soap opera *As the World Turns*. He let me into the VIP room, but I still couldn't afford the drinks. A few weeks later my character ended up being murdered by his own grandmother anyway.

Sitting at my desk across from the indomitable Ben Kennedy with his stupid haircut, I realized that, sure, our backgrounds were different. We were like kids from the opposite side of the tracks in a John Hughes movie, *The Breakfast Club* or *Pretty in Pink*—but maybe what motivated us was actually the same. For each of us, "no deals equaled no paycheck"—and who knows what that meant for Ben? Maybe it meant he'd have no money to pay his bills and could end up homeless or move back to a hometown that only had one traffic light. I had no idea. But, like me, Ben didn't seem to want to look back—just forward, and that meant we both needed to make sales.

I wanted to stay in New York City, the land where dreams are made amongst the noise and crowds. Moving back to Colorado, where my parents had moved after I went to college, conjured up some frightening images—me working as a ranch hand, painting a never-ending fence. Then I'd marry a winsome cowgirl, have a few kids—buy a tractor, maybe get a dog and a few chickens…and then die. I wanted bigger and better things for myself. I wanted to reach my full potential, and that meant doing whatever it would take to stay in New York City. Maybe I had reached my full potential as an actor, but I certainly hadn't reached my full potential as a human being. Landing a role on a soap opera after having auditioned for an internet reality show called *InTurn*, where I fought to actor-death with twelve other costars to be the next soap star on *As the World Turns*, takes initiative! And couldn't I use initiative to jump-start my career in sales?

I thought about how I could take initiative to move my career forward every day. I asked more experienced brokers if I could shadow them for a day or run one of their open houses. I put more ads on Craigslist. I worked to be less shy. Soon I started to feel less weird about not going to auditions, and more excited about selling. It was a slow, steady process. There were occasional bumps, big and small, but I kept going. At first, I was fueled by fear and the scary thoughts of returning home to Colorado a failure. As I started making more deals, my motivation began to shift. It morphed from "I hope I do enough rentals this month so that I can pay rent and buy a new shirt," to "Wow. I just deposited a commission check that will cover my rent for two years. What else am I capable of?" The hardest thing for me to teach my new sales agents at Team Serhant is how powerful taking initiative really is. It might sound crazy, but those moments when you feel stuck? Like you'll never close a sale or get another client again? Initiative is like a magical cure-all elixir. Pick up the phone and make a call, send an email, follow up with leads. Do something. Taking initiative is like breathing for a salesperson; you cannot survive without it. Take initiative with everything that is put in front of you, and you will experience success every single day.

When I got serious about selling real estate I wanted to succeed, but I felt handicapped by the fact that I wasn't from New York City. I didn't know many people. Who exactly was I going to sell real estate to? And I didn't have the same in-depth knowledge of the different neighborhoods that a native would. After taking initiative, very often self-doubt sets in. But, once again, my previous life as an actor ended up being a secret weapon. As an actor, I wasn't fazed by rejection, I was good at reading people, and I could quickly memorize things like facts about buildings. My goofy personality and prematurely grey hair actually won some people over.

It doesn't matter if you have a different background than others in your industry. Don't get hindered by self-doubt. Being different can be good. Your skills—whether in the culinary arts, sports, or teaching—add value to your character. If you can manage a class of unruly seventh graders or perform a physical examination on a snake, you can dominate at sales. Who you were before you entered sales matters. Your personality needs to be authentic to you, even if it's quirky. I have very successful team members who tended bar, were in the military, worked in banking, etc. Each one of them has a unique body of knowledge and brings their own fresh perspective to their sales practice. Their prior work experience ultimately makes them more interesting and well-rounded people, and it's the same for you. Embrace who you are and think about how your skills can enhance your sales career.

I've wanted to be successful since I was about four years old. Did I have any clue about how I was going to make that happen? None whatsoever. My skill set at that age consisted of a few lame magic tricks and a couple of knock-knock jokes. It turns out that choosing success first—and letting the career follow—was one of the best things I could have done for myself. It forced me to be open about how that success would come—because it turns out that I wasn't going to have it as an actor. When that dream died, my desire to be successful didn't wither away with it. I was still committed to the idea of success, I just needed to plug into a different route to get there. Most people hit a bump along the way and they think, *Okay, it's all over for me!*, but that's not true. If you are committed to being successful no matter what, those bumps don't matter—you've decided on your final destination and you'll do whatever it takes to get there.

Serhant Secret #2

Choose success first, no matter what—
then back yourself into a career.

ENDURANCE FOR THE WIN

Every year, over 50,000 runners come from all over the world to participate in the New York City marathon, as if running 26.2 miles isn't that big a deal. Do you know what happened to the first guy who ran a marathon? He dropped dead. Okay, so that was in Greece, where it is super hot, and it was in the year 490 BC. There were no running shoes or water bottles for easy hydration. Now practically anyone can run a marathon with the right preparation. You train carefully, increase your mileage, eat well—and then put your name on a T-shirt in big glittery letters so when the crowd shouts, "GO, RYAN," you force yourself to keep moving instead of sitting down on the curb and ordering a pizza. With the proper training, it's possible to cross the finish line and live to Instagram about it. But what if, after all that preparation, the race suddenly switched from a marathon to a sprint? You'd been running slowly and steadily, and now for some unexpected reason you have to hustle like hell to get to the finish line? You start to increase your speed, you're doing it—but wait, stop! Never mind! We're going back to the really long and drawn-out race...and good luck to you!

Whether you're in sales for an employer or you're an entrepreneur, you know exactly what I'm talking about. There are the crazy long deals stretched out over what feels like years, a humble pilgrimage to the end result. And there are the deals that are lightning quick, where you feel like a genie—you nod and there's the prize. Then there are the ones that switch back and forth, nearly sucking you dry of energy and sanity. Sales requires a tremendous amount of endurance, and training yourself to be ready for any kind of deal will give you a gigantic edge over your competitors. Balls up!

Sales is like a race, except no one is going to tell you what kind of race it is until that gun goes off. As you start to sell more, it becomes clear that success is about how hard you work—it's about your endurance, it's about your ability to sustain a lot of balls. The more ads I placed, the more showings I did, the more connections I made—the more I sold. It wasn't like acting; no one ever said, "I'm not taking this well-priced-spacious-apartment-that's-perfect-for-me-in-every-way because I don't like your face." Sales is about the work, simple as that.

The best thing about selling is that you can do whatever you want to increase your stamina, survive that race, and cross the finish line. No one is telling you to punch out. The choice is yours. You decide how hard you want to work and how much money you make. No salesperson ever got a call like, "Hi. This is Pam, you know, from HR? I have to tell you that you sold way too much this month. Your sales were, like, way over the top—and exceeded everyone else's. You're making too much money for this company. Consider this a warning." Am I right?

Early in my career, no matter what was thrown at me, I wasn't going to stop. That put me at a competitive advantage over my colleagues. While other brokers were going on vacation, in the Hamptons for the weekend, at a movie, out for dinner, or sleeping, I would be hard at work, ready to surge ahead of them. Sales is a crazy race. While they were taking a hot yoga class or eating sushi with friends, I was checking off my to-do list.

THE SIX RULES
TO MORE SALES

1. Never hyper-focus on one ball. You do not live or die by one sale.
2. You never wonder, "What's next?" because your next deal is already in the works.
3. You are surrounded by opportunity—making contacts, gaining referrals, generating new business, always reaching for new balls.
4. You know that it takes as much energy to manage one ball as it does four, five, or even six.
5. You control the flight path—you know which balls to handle first, which ones to deal with quickly, and which ones require more time and attention.
6. You don't blindly toss balls in the air. You care about where each one lands.

LET FEAR DRIVE YOUR SUCCESS

It's 4:53 on a cold Tuesday morning in December, and I'm trying to decide which cool new headband I should wear to the gym. While I'm debating between the pink and the purple, it becomes harder to ignore the thoughts that are swirling through my head. These thoughts have been known to include, but are not limited to: *What if Manhattan blows up? What if Emilia gets mad at me for working too much? What if I fall and shatter my pelvis and can't show apartments? What if I'm pulled in too many directions and my team decides they've all had it? I think I'm getting a cold—is this a cold?? Or is it the flu, like the weird kind you catch from a bird and you die? You know what would be so embarrassing? If no one bought my book except my parents.*

I wake up afraid. Every day. But my fear is my most powerful source of fuel. It drives me forward unlike anything else. The life I've built for myself (The Serhant Team, two TV shows on Bravo, my vlog on YouTube, my beautiful homes, and a wife who is even more beautiful and lovely) looks very different than it did on the day I started my career as a real estate broker. As I mentioned, it was September 15, 2008, the day Lehman Brothers announced they would file for bankruptcy, triggering the collapse of the world economy. A feeling of uncertainty permeated everything, and it was really hard to feel optimistic about my new job. After I left the office that day, I popped into the Food Emporium to buy my favorite sources of cheap protein—tofu and yogurt. I gave my credit card to the cashier. A few seconds later, he handed it back. DECLINED. My heart dropped. I muttered something about getting cash and ran out of the store. I jumped on the subway, sat down, and started to cry. I literally didn't have enough money to buy a container of cheap yogurt. I haven't let myself forget what I felt like that day—broke and afraid, and like I couldn't make it on my own. It lit a fire in me. Every deal I make, every project I go after, and every extra-long day I work is to distance myself as far as I can from that moment.

Know what your motivation is. Connect with that one thing that motivates you from deep in your core. It can be life-changing. It's not enough to say, "I want to be awesome and make a lot of money." Who doesn't want that? Think about what really pushes you to work harder and do better. What motivates you so deeply that it can provide you with that extra boost of power to send your career into overdrive? Don't let what scares you keep you up at night; make it push you to reach an insane level of success instead.

NONE OF THIS WORKS WITHOUT CONFIDENCE

I'm a very confident person. Hence, the name of my book. It took a long time, but I can say without hesitation that I'm a great salesperson. If I let fear rule over everything, I'd be too scared to make a cold call or have a conversation with a new client. It's that touch of fear that keeps everything in balance. But you can't sit on the confidence side of the seesaw forever. You'll get stuck in a routine, and this is the real death of a salesman. It also puts you at risk of becoming an overconfident, arrogant asshole. And that's gross.

It's usually after my daily workouts that my confidence surges back. I start to think about the challenges of the day: coaching a Japanese couple through a co-op interview for a $31 million apartment, and dealing with a square footage discrepancy in a $16 million loft in SoHo my client is supposed to close on tomorrow. Ten years ago, my biggest problems were making rent and getting into the shower before Jun Woo and Ha Rin used up all the hot water.* Now my challenges force me to stretch, and be more confident. I have no choice but to figure out the best way to steer my ship forward. The questions, problems, doubts, and fears don't necessarily vanish—they grow along with me. So, when I think back to the shit show that was my early career, I'm thankful for what Ben Kennedy did for me. He didn't show me how to rent an apartment, but he showed me what happens when you face your fears head-on—you become unstoppable.

Every morning, after checking my calendar, I'm ready to go. I kiss my sleeping wife goodbye and pop in my earbuds. Just as the elevator doors open, I take a breath, step in, and say my mantra, "Ready, set, GO," knowing I'm ready to face whatever kind of race today throws my way.

---

* Their names were printed on a giant smiley face poster they kept on their door. That's how I remember them.

THE SERHANT WAY

You've made the decision to transform yourself into a selling machine, and that's awesome. Just remember that no one will hand you a road map for your own success! Trust me, you're *already* an amazing salesperson—you just may not know it yet. All the tools you need to succeed in sales are within you; it's just a matter of finding them and putting them to work. Today, use the information in this book to point yourself toward greater success. Decide now that you will take your sales to unimaginable heights. You're already off to a great start because you're now taking more initiative to create change! From now on, initiative will seep from your pores. Don't stop there. Make endurance your middle name (well, not literally) by outlasting and outselling your competition. And if this all scares you a little bit? So what? Let that fear be the fuel that drives you straight down the path to success.

You've got to:

- Take initiative. What does initiative look like to you?
- Dig deep, and find the endurance you need to make it over the finish line.
- Let your fear push you toward success.
- Never forget: none of this works without confidence.

CHAPTER 2

The Power of Yes

To: desperaterealtor@ryanserhant.com
From: possiblyfake@maybespam.com
Re: Investment!

Dear Sirs:

I am seeking help to make a big real estate investment in New York City. Please respond if you can help me make this investment.

Yours truly,
"Mr. X of Atlantis"*

Looking back, this email sounds very spammy. But Mr. X wasn't offering discount Viagra, and he wasn't asking for any help transferring his billions of dollars into America via my personal bank account. This was very early on in my career and at this point I was very eager for more balls, sooo...I answered it.

---

* I *know* Atlantis is a made-up place. I'm hiding Mr. X's true identity to avoid getting myself killed.

"Yes! Of course I can help you find an apartment!"

I had no idea when I hit SEND that I was putting myself first in line to ride the world's scariest and most outrageous sales roller coaster.

I emailed back and forth with Mr. X, to get to know him a bit and get a better sense of what he was looking for. When he said he "worked in energy," it was like someone had stabbed me with a sharp red flag that read, "This guy is totally fake or a drug dealer. Run away *now*." But I didn't. Instead I did a quick Google search and got just enough evidence to think he was real. Maybe. His name was linked to a very expensive house outside Paris. If he could afford that, there was a chance he was legit and I could make the biggest sale of my career. I had hope. I was in. I said yes.

I had just the right listing, and it was my biggest listing to date. A spectacular four-bedroom apartment in Midtown with a den and a separate dining room that was listed for $8.5 million. After looking at pictures and a video of the apartment he offered $8 million, and after some negotiating with the sellers we agreed to $8.2 million. Done! I couldn't believe it. After months of doing rentals I had just sold a super expensive apartment over the internet to a guy who cold-emailed me. Nothing shady about that whatsoever. I took myself out for a very lavish dinner to celebrate. All I had to do next was get a couple of signatures, a deposit, and close the deal. Right? And that's when the story of a simple real estate transaction turns into a Michael Bay movie—featuring my career and ego nearly going down in an Armageddon-style explosion of flames.

Mr. X vanished. He wasn't answering my calls, emails, or texts. I had no idea where he was or how to reach him. I had just convinced my sellers to accept an offer from someone who in reality might be a twelve-year-old hacker who was laughing at me from his Spider-Man bedroom somewhere in the Midwest. Or maybe he was a pirate. I didn't really know. I was starting to regret ordering that expensive bottle of wine at dinner. Why hadn't I just ordered takeout? The sellers were getting itchy to get the contract signed, and I was increasingly nervous about who I had "sold" this apartment to. I didn't want to let my sellers down. I had made a personal commitment to them. As a salesman, your word is your bond. Telling them, "Oh sorry. Turns out that the buyer isn't a wealthy foreigner but is actually a member of a child-run computer hacking gang," wasn't an option. The truth was I just wasn't sure. If I was 100 percent positive the buyer was fake, then I would have to fess up and deal with the consequences. But this buyer was the only one I had, and until I knew for sure he wasn't real I was going to do everything in my power to make this deal happen. So, I sent a dramatic and somewhat risky email:

> I know you spend your time mostly in Atlantis dealing with "energy" and you mentioned you have a home in Paris, so I'll be coming through Paris and would love to close this deal if you perhaps have a free second and aren't actually a criminal trying to steal my identity.

He wrote back immediately:

> LOL. How's tomorrow?

Face time matters in sales. Whenever I have a client who is on the fence about a deal, or hesitating to move forward, I schedule a face-to-face meeting right away. People often struggle to make decisions, and if they're not in front of you it's out of sight and out of mind. It's easy to ignore texts and emails, but it's not easy to ignore someone sitting right across from you. I take in-person meetings whenever I can. An in-person meeting shows a client your level of commitment. In the end you'll also save time, close more sales, and be ready to tackle that next ball.

Serhant Secret #3

Never underestimate the power of a face-to-face meeting. Sometimes emails and texts are not enough to get a deal closed.

Did I mention that I didn't really have plans to fly to Paris? I did now. I wanted to show this buyer/pirate/drug dealer that I was totally committed to him and closing the deal. I was hungry for this sale. Literally, because I was about to spend my last few thousand dollars flying to Paris to meet with a potential client (or criminal). I didn't even pack a bag. I put on a suit and boarded the plane with nothing other than the contract and his alleged address in Paris. I was nervous. Mr. X knew I was coming, but I didn't have an official appointment. When I tried to look up his address, it appeared his office was located in an empty parking lot or behind a French car dealership. Nothing suspicious about that! When I arrived in Paris the next morning after a long, uncomfortable flight, I took a taxi to the address he gave me. It did exist! But don't get too excited. No one was there, and from the looks of the place, it didn't seem like anyone had been there in a long time. I hadn't flown all this way stuffed between two snoring tourists for nothing, so I sat down on his stoop and waited. And got a macaron. Then waited some more. Then I decided, "Hey, I guess I'll get a croissant." I charged my phone somewhere, got another macaron. Waiting. Repeat. As the day went on I started to feel depressed. I had just made a total fool of myself. My emotions ran from anger at myself to embarrassment. Why am I so stupid??!!! Then I hit the lowest of lows. I felt truly unworthy of being a broker. Why do all of the other brokers have such an easy time making deals and I don't? As I sat on that stoop feeling sorry for myself, I thought about what I would tell people when I got back. Like, "Oh, it was a great trip but he had to run off to Zanzibar to buy an elephant, so he couldn't see me." Or maybe I'd go with, "His busy pirate schedule of looting ships in international waters prevented us from having dinner." Or, worst of all, "His mom doesn't let him go out with strangers or buy multimillion-dollar apartments because he's actually a child." But then something happened. I got an email with the address of a bar where he was hanging out. He wanted me to meet him there. I felt like I had opened a chocolate bar and found the last golden ticket. He. Was. Real.

Mr. X turned out to be a fairly normal guy who just happened to be flanked by a team of bodyguards. He had an assistant whose sole job was to bring him espresso. He mostly wanted to chill and drink $700 bottles of vodka—preferably until 3 a.m. That's great, but I was there to get a contract signed, and he didn't even want to talk about it. Mr. X clearly enjoyed watching the preppy guy squirm. It was like a game to him, and he was setting the rules. "Will you at least read this if I do another shot?" I begged. Not how I normally do business, but what did I have to lose other than my reputation and my career?

Just as I was starting to see double, he agreed to read the contract. "Why do I need to provide all this personal information? Do these people in New York not want my cash?" he asked. The people in New York definitely wanted his cash, but like trophy wives, New York wanted that cash on its own terms. After hours of drinking I was still able to switch on my inner salesman and flip what he viewed as a negative into a positive. I confidently told him, "It's standard in NYC. Everyone must fill out the same paperwork. It keeps the city safer." He seemed to buy that, but he didn't sign the contract. It was many shots and several hours later that I staggered out of that bar with a signed contract in my hand. It was a win, but a temporary one. I got back to New York to find that Mr. X hadn't sent the deposit. A contract without a deposit is essentially a worthless piece of paper. It means nothing. Where was the 10 percent of the $8.2 million? Was he planning to ship the cash over in bags like in an old Western bank robbery movie? About a million phone calls and several near heart attacks later, I got a call from the lawyer while I was sitting in a taxi, stuck in traffic. A wire of $820,000 from Mr. X had just arrived. And breathe…

Fast-forward to Mr. X's closing. It had been weeks since I'd heard from him and I was worried that he wasn't going to come through. This ball had been in my pocket for a long time and I was ready to be finished with it. The day of the closing I got a text:

Meet me at the Mandarin Oriental. Now.

Oh my God. He's here in NYC! Amazing. On the other hand, seriously? What a dick. But I made it uptown in record time. Then I sat in the lobby waiting. For an hour. As I waited I reminded myself that he was making the rules for this deal and if I played his game I'd reap a big reward on the other end. Remember, this was my listing, and this was a direct client, so the commission was 6 percent of $8.2 million (that's $492,000). That was more money than I thought I'd ever make in my entire career, let alone in one deal with a pirate!

Sales can mean playing games where you don't get to make the rules. My persistence with Mr. X would only work out if I was able to keep my ego in check and let him lead the way. As salespeople, we must be careful listeners, because clients are always sending messages about what they need and how they want to conduct business. In this case, the disappearing, lateness, and last-minute text messages said, "I am totally in charge. We're doing this on my terms and I'll sign papers, send money, and close when I feel like it." This was a game, and if I wanted to win I needed to go along with it whether I liked it or not. Sure, I could have objected to this way of doing business, but would that have changed anything? It probably would have meant losing the sale and that was not an option. Never forget that while you're a salesperson, you are also in the service business—and sometimes that means being flexible and playing by someone else's rules.

Serhant Secret #4

Closing a deal means keeping your ego in check
at all times.

He finally came to the lobby with an entourage of bodyguards and assistants and we all piled into a fleet of black SUVs. I felt just like a Secret Service man (but without a gun, lifesaving self-defense skills, or cool sunglasses).

We start moving through the Manhattan traffic, and it's taking forever. But then wait a minute…why are we going through the tunnel headed for the highway? The closing is just downtown! All my fears surrounding the shadiness of this deal come flooding back with a vengeance. *Are they planning to harvest my organs? Am I being kidnapped? Am I going to be sold as a sex slave?* Just as I'm texting my mother about my imminent death I notice we are at JFK. It's obvious I'm about to be taken hostage. We pull up to a black 747 and Mr. X gets out. A man approaches holding a bottle of champagne on a silver tray. What. Is. Happening?! Mr. X speaks to the man, signs a piece of paper, and gets back into the car and announces, "Now I am ready to go to the closing." No big deal. He just bought a 747 on the *way to his closing*! After I regained consciousness and my blood pressure returned to normal, we headed back to Manhattan and closed the biggest deal of my career. Next ball, please!

SAYING YES = SELLING MORE

Looking back at this story, I admit it does sound bananas. To fly across the ocean to find someone who may or may not exist and get him to sign papers. But in the end, the story isn't about me dropping everything to sit around and drink café au lait all day—it's about a deep commitment to closing a deal. No matter how big or how small (or how crazy), I will do everything in my power to make a deal happen. And what I didn't understand while I was eating my third croissant was that maybe other brokers only say yes to the easy deals. Maybe that's why I was struggling while other brokers seemed to be moving through deals with little effort. It's easy to say *no*. It's easy to make excuses about why you can't close a deal. It's much easier to focus on what could go wrong or what the immediate challenges are—but none of that stopped me from saying *yes*.

Serhant Secret #5

There will be an objection with almost every single sale.
The goal is to turn negatives into positives.

Sure, maybe people thought I was crazy to chase down a possible pirate. But you know what? When people think you're crazy it's just because they don't have the courage to do what you're doing. And who cares what other people think? It's your career, your vision, and it's your commission. Just a few years later I'm still riding that roller coaster with Mr. X, and it's soaring to new heights. His real estate portfolio is worth over $250 million, and guess who sold him all that property? I did. The wild ride was worth it.

I've said yes to many things: doing a reality TV show, selling a haunted brownstone, taking on listings that have been sitting on the market for ages, representing clients who have fired 15 other brokers, opening a Brooklyn office in two weeks so I could sell a large inventory of houses in a new market. The list goes on, and the only thing I've said NO to was having a live tiger at an open house—that's just going too far. But it was that first big deal with Mr. X that showed me the true power of YES when it comes to making volume sales. I sell more because I say YES when other people would say no, and I can keep moving a client forward until that deal is done. Saying yes to every opportunity was my way of believing in myself and showing everyone I was the best—even when I wasn't. I've also learned that quickly flipping negatives into positives will help you close deals faster and more frequently. Sometimes this is as simple as asking yourself, "Is this negative really even a negative?" For example, if I'm selling an apartment with no light I'll push this as a positive to a client who is almost never home, or only home at night. Why pay for a view you won't even see? Take the time to think about the usual objections you have in your area of sales; it's likely you'll hear the same objections over and over. How can you show clients that this isn't really a negative? How can you turn this around? Anticipating objections and immediately turning them into positives will result in you selling more. Get ready to juggle more balls and cash bigger checks!

AN UNEXPECTED SALES WEAPON: IMPROV

If you visited my office on a random Monday morning during our team meeting, you might think you had mistakenly walked into a circus or a lunatic asylum. You might see a normal-looking guy in a nice suit saying something like, "Look! It's raining Oreos again!," while the woman next to him barks like a dog, and the broker next to her flaps pretend wings while singing a country and western song. Don't be afraid. It's just our team improv workshop. Everyone on my team takes improv. Practicing improv is one of our secret weapons in becoming sales machines. When I started doing improv as a high school dork I never imagined it would be so useful when I became a salesperson. Improv builds synergy and teaches your mind to constantly fire away in a positive direction. Improv is all about YES, and taking that yes forward and adding onto it. NO is forbidden in improv, as it should be in sales. If someone says, "Elephants give birth to pineapples." You can't say "What? Do you really think that?" as you carefully back away from the insane person. The rule is you have to say *"Yes! And they have six legs!"* Nothing is wrong. Everything and anything is possible!

YES is the most essential word in any salesperson's vocabulary. Say yes to opportunities so that you have lots of balls to play with. You have to persuade clients to say yes to making purchases. You have to say yes to taking risks. And maybe most importantly, if a client were to say, "I only want to buy from the best shoe salesperson in the world. Is that you?" don't hesitate to shout, *"Yes, I am the best!"* from the top of the nearest mountain. Or just climb on a chair, you know, whatever works. When you are asked to do something new or totally foreign to you and you have no idea how to do it, say YES and trust yourself to figure out how to do it later. This automatically puts you ahead of every other salesperson who said NO. I really figured out how to be a broker when I was cast on *Million Dollar Listing New York*. I was a very new broker when I went to an open casting call with 3,000 other agents at the Hudson Hotel in early 2010. When the casting director called me a few months later and said they liked my audition and wanted me to come back in, I didn't say "I'll pass. I don't have much experience," even though being on a national television show would be a huge platform for sales. That would have been a loss of an amazing opportunity, one that has resulted in many balls being tossed my way. When your instant reaction to everything is no, it's like you're unleashing a little monster that eats up all of life's possibilities.

EVERY DEAL IS ANOTHER SCENE

Improv requires careful listening. If your partner says, "Bathing in a pit of spiders is super fun," it's your job to add a witty retort like, "Yes, *and* it's my go-to cure for a bad hangover." But if you weren't listening and you have no idea what she said, you'll miss out on the opportunity to add to that narrative (and you'll just look like an idiot). A sale is ultimately another narrative. It's a story. And if you want to control the direction the narrative goes (ideally toward closing and a nice big check), you need to listen to what your client is saying to you. You can't be a one-note salesperson. Not everyone responds to the same song, and it's your job to adjust the tune and play the right notes. You have to constantly ask yourself, "What does this client need from me?" and respond at their level. Ask yourself:

- Is there something I can do right this second to make my client's life easier? Do I need to schedule appointments at a time that's more convenient for her, even if that means early mornings or late nights?
- Does this person need a friend? I'm not saying become their best friend in, like, a weird way. But is this process new to your client? Do they need more handholding?
- Does your client need to be gently prodded into action? Are they only going to make a move if they think the window of opportunity to buy what you are selling is about to slam shut?

Practice listening to your clients before you talk. Take a few seconds to digest what they are saying before you respond. Think about what they are saying to you first, and be sincere when you speak. There is nothing worse than spouting a line, just to fill up the silence. That doesn't help. You end up sounding like a bad actor who has memorized his lines and only speaks when he's given the right cue. Model yourself after an Academy Award winner! Great actors speak a scripted line and manage to sound like those words have never been said before. They can take a person along on an emotional journey that results in tears, fear, or laughter. No one will cry when a bad actor awkwardly blurts out in a monotone voice, "Oh, no, my mother. She is gone. Whatever will I do now?" I am *not* telling you to put on a character; you must be genuine. But don't be afraid to dig deep and elicit emotion when necessary. That's how a good salesperson makes sure he is giving a client what he needs to end the story with a big sale.

Nine Reasons to Sign Up for an Improv Workshop NOW*

1. Improv opens you up so that you can make genuine connections with people. You'll feel more comfortable and secure talking to new people.
2. Improv will help you think quickly on your feet. You'll instantly be able to come up with a solution to any problem or any objection a client might have.
3. When you practice improv, your brain is always firing YES. Not making a deal—not getting to a place of yes—is no longer an option.
4. Practicing improv will quickly show you what your strengths and weaknesses are.
5. You learn to relate to your scene partner, and, ultimately, every deal is just another scene.
6. Improv forces you to listen before you react. Listening to your clients and hearing what they want are key to closing sales.
7. When you get really good at improv, you can control the narrative. You can use this skill to control the direction of your deals.
8. Improv can help conquer shyness.
9. It's hilarious.

---

* If you live somewhere like the North Pole where the improv offerings are scarce, please don't give up. Force your family and friends to practice with you, or start your own group with other salespeople! Please, I'm serious. Improv can be the secret ingredient that boosts your sales to an entirely new level of awesome. And P.S. Shakespeare was an excellent roller skater!

PLANET CONFIDENCE:
WHERE EVERYONE WANTS WHAT YOU'RE SELLING

I'm all about saying yes to more balls. But a big part of turning those balls into closed sales and big commission checks is about getting clients to say YES to what you're selling. I can't tell you how many times a member of The Scrhant Team has walked into my office and asked me to speak to a client, because "They'll feel more comfortable hearing it from me" or "They'll believe it if they hear it directly from Ryan."

I'm always happy to help out—I want my team to succeed and the brokers I work with to grow. But the truth is, clients aren't accepting my word because I'm some powerful wizard— I'm not the Oz of real estate. Buyers and sellers accept what I'm saying because I speak from a place of complete confidence. My confidence assures people that when I say things like, "This is a fantastic apartment; I think you should snap it up," it's true, and they should buy it. Not next week or next month—but today. If you want a client to buy what you are selling, self-confidence needs to be oozing out of your pores.

You must decide that there is no choice but to be the BEST salesperson that has ever existed in the history of the entire universe. Early on in my career, I bought myself a one-way ticket to planet confidence and I've never looked back. Am I joking when I say I'm the best broker in the history of the entire universe? Sure, kind of. That is a ridiculous statement to make. Does it mean I don't make mistakes or don't have more to learn? Definitely not. But I do know that I'll work more and fight harder than anyone else, and do absolutely everything in my power to get a deal done and make my clients happy. And in my book, that's what makes me the best. You might be the best salesperson for totally different reasons, and that's awesome.

ONE RISK AT A TIME

Today I can walk into a boardroom with a table as long as the Brooklyn Bridge and introduce myself as "the best broker in the world,"* but I still remember what it feels like to be the new guy on the block. Literally. My family moved a ton when I was a kid. It was never easy to have to start over at a new school, not knowing anyone at all. Meeting people as an adult is hard enough, but as a kid it's *the worst*. When we first arrived in Massachusetts, my dad announced to my little brother Jack and me that it was "time to go make some friends." He had a plan. We were going to walk up and down Hill Street in Topsfield, knocking on every single door to introduce ourselves. We were like, um, *why*? Looking back, it was a great idea. But at the time, my fifth-grade self couldn't imagine anything more terrifying. My dad told us, "What's the worst thing that can happen? Someone laughs or slams the door in our faces? Then that neighbor is crazy and we'll stay away. Or, you could meet a lot of nice people and maybe even your new best friend."

I was so scared that I can't really remember going to houses

---

* If you're thinking, "He's the best broker in the world? Well, duh, he's *on TV*," sure, being on TV is a big advantage—it opens lots of doors. But when I take new business meetings I have to assure people I will do a good job *despite* being on TV.

one and two. They are a complete blur. House number three was different. We met the Badavas family. They were friendly and super cool, and my brother and I were like, "Oh my God. Dad was right!" At that moment, a switch flipped in my mind. My fear turned into a game—and I wanted to win. "How many doors can we knock on? How many friends can I have in my pocket by the end of the day?" Sure, knocking on doors with my dad made life easier for a shy fifth grader at a new school, but the ultimate lesson was much bigger than that. I learned that taking a risk is doable. Had I not gone along with my dad's plan, I would have walked into school on the first day not knowing a single person. But because I took a risk, I had automatically put myself in a better position to succeed, or at the very least I wouldn't have to sit alone in the cafeteria on the first day of school like a freak.

It's the same with sales. Sure, risks can be scary—cold calls, meeting new people, pitching new clients, mixing up your usual sales pitch. Or you can push fear aside and focus on the reward that might be waiting on the other side of the door. New clients, more deals, and bigger sales? What's the reward you want? Doubling your sales? Selling a new product? Trying out a new territory? Making enough money to pay for your kids' college or take your dream vacation? The Serhants and the Badavas family have been lifelong friends since the day we showed up at their front door. I never could have imagined such a risk would pay off in such a good way. If there's the possibility of that big reward on the other side of the door, just knock on it. Go ahead, take a risk. What are you waiting for? See? You're still alive! Take another one. Then do it again.

A CONFESSION: SHYNESS SUCKS

I can walk into a room and tell anyone that I'm the greatest salesperson in the universe. But that doesn't mean I just tossed off my shyness like a dirty gym T-shirt. It's still something I have to work on even to this day. Last Friday I found myself in a room full of people I didn't know. And I hated it. I was meeting Emilia at a gala for the Hellenic Initiative, a cause that's important to her. I arrived before she did and found myself in a giant room full of Greeks. They were all happily chatting in groups, like they had all known each other for decades. My first instinct was to stand in the corner alone and look at my phone, or, better yet, leave (but then my wife would kill me). I got a glass of champagne from the bar and started awkwardly circling the room while glancing at my phone to see if there were any exciting news stories (there weren't). After half an hour of roaming the room like a weirdo, I finally had to encourage myself to jump in the water. I didn't want to—I knew it would be cold and uncomfortable. But I forced myself to walk up to whoever was closest to me and that was the photographer who was shooting the event. I decided to go with "Hi, I'm Ryan," as my brilliant opener. We chatted for a few minutes and he showed me a few pictures of his kids. Okay, I didn't sink—I survived that initial plunge and was ready to dive deeper. Then the photographer introduced me to some people he knew, and they were nice and happy to talk to me. Things got better, and I was able to tread water quite easily and then my brother-in-law showed up. I've never been happier to see him. I didn't drown, and chances are that no one ever has died from introducing themselves to a stranger at a social event.

Many years after we walked down the street knocking on doors, my family moved again, this time to Colorado. I was already in college, so I didn't have to worry about making new friends again, but my little brother was in high school. He had to start from scratch. He was nervous, as any high school kid would be, but I was excited for him. High school wasn't easy for me. Even though I had found the theatre, I was never really comfortable in my own skin. I wasn't a jock and I wasn't super smart. I was the kid who liked to recite poetry and wear loud Hawaiian shirts Every. Single. Day. If I could send high school Ryan a message from future Ryan, it would be this: Ditch the shyness. Don't be afraid to take risks; you have nothing to lose. Poetry and Hawaiian shirts are awesome and it doesn't matter that you aren't on the hockey team. Ask out any girl you want! I told all of this to my brother. He took that advice to heart and became one of the most popular kids in his high school (although he did dress better than I did).

We are salespeople—that means we have to talk to people and meet people all the time. We must always be on the lookout for opportunities because anyone anywhere can be our next best customer. I still have to remind myself that my next big client could be that complete stranger I'm too afraid to talk to at a party—and that I should put my phone down and get out of the corner. I know that no matter what heights I hit in my career, the first move is always going to be hard to make. But I'm never going to let that stop me. So the next time you feel apprehensive about taking a risk, just remember that in the end, putting your phone in your pocket, getting out of that corner, and letting the world see how awesome you really are can take you somewhere bigger and better than you'd ever thought you'd go.

And don't you want to see where your story will take you?

THE SERHANT WAY

Saying YES = Selling More. Don't be afraid to say yes, even if you're not sure what you're doing or where to start. You'd be surprised how many salespeople say no to an opportunity just because the idea of stepping into uncharted territory makes them uncomfortable. Saying yes gives you an enormous advantage over your competition. But I understand how terrifying it can be to say yes: I've said yes to many opportunities and those that frightened me often turned out to be the most rewarding—financially and emotionally. Don't forget you have the power to figure things out. And if someone thinks you're crazy for saying yes? Even better! They don't have the courage to do what you're doing.

Remember that getting to YES can mean:

- Playing by someone else's rules.
- Learning to quickly turn negatives into positives.

Keep building your confidence.

- An improv class can give you an edge—it's a secret sales weapon.
- Your confidence will build with each risk you take.

PRACTICE YOUR CRAFT

This entire book is about priming your mind so that you can be the best salesperson, but I've also included a few exercises. There is no circumstance where you would do any of these with a customer in real life. It's practice! I jump on top of boxes at the gym to improve my "explosiveness." I'm not going to leap on top of a dinner table to show off my explosiveness to a client—that would be insane. These exercises are tools and they are fun. Salespeople who are better at being human sell more stuff. It's true! It wasn't a surprise that my past life as an actor helped prepare me for the world of reality television. All the auditions, plays, student films, and, of course, playing Dr. Evan Walsh made it easier for me to adapt to life with television cameras in my personal spaces, such as my car, office, bedroom, and shower. You do not need to be an actor—it doesn't matter if you were never even in a high school musical—but know that some of the crazy exercises I'm sharing in this book are similar to ones actors use. I've included them in this book because they will make you a better human.

THE QUESTION GAME

I'm sure you've already signed up for a local improv class, and you're loving it and can't wait for your family and friends to come see your first show—you're the next Tina Fey! But just in case you want to practice on those nights that the Improv Dungeon is closed, I thought I'd leave you with an exercise. You're welcome!

Asking questions—and then *more* questions—is an invaluable skill for a salesperson to have in her arsenal. Think about it! If someone asks you, "So, how are you feeling today?" and you reply, "I feel awesome," and you just leave it at that, you're basically signaling to them that the conversation is over, and P.S. you don't care about how they feel. That isn't exactly the kind of interaction that promotes connection and sales. To make sure you don't find yourself falling into a dead-end conversation with a customer, practice The Question Game. Make your friends or family—or your Uber driver—do it with you. It's a simple game (but oh so hard!).

How to play:

Set your timer for two minutes (once you become a master of this game, do it for longer). Start a conversation with the other person by asking them a question. They must reply to your question with, you guessed it, another question. Continue this for the entire two minutes. Whoever messes up and answers a question with a statement loses the game.

CHAPTER 3

Work for the Deal

When I met Linus at an open house on East 36th Street, I thought he was kind of peculiar, possibly insane. While all the other guys were wearing suits and looked like they belonged in the corner office of a law firm, Linus was wearing a rumpled, bright purple tracksuit and his hair stuck straight up in tufts of grey and black. Though his appearance was bananas, he had an air of confidence about him, and his mannerisms, while odd, also suggested he felt at home in the $4.5 million apartment we were standing in.

He wasn't talking to anyone so I introduced myself, even though he looked like someone's crazy uncle. I complimented him on his vibrant color choices. Purple is my favorite color. We chatted about how we both like theatre. I handed him my business card and figured I'd never hear from purple tracksuit guy ever again. Except he called me the next day. He said I seemed nice, and knowledgeable about the market. He wanted me to show him some apartments in Manhattan. I never judge a book by its cover—Linus's cover featured a jarring, creepy grin topped with Einstein hair—but he was also a potential $4–$5 million buyer.

I had just listed a house in Park Slope, Brooklyn, that I loved.

The detail of the restoration, the big bedrooms, the marble kitchen—all were exquisite. Linus wanted an apartment in Manhattan (and also maybe to recruit me into a freaky cult), but my gut told me he'd love the Park Slope house as much as I did.

When I told him about the house, he said, "I'm scared of houses and Brooklyn," but to his credit he agreed to check it out. It's not often that I meet a client in Murray Hill who agrees to see a property all the way in Park Slope. But it's not often I meet a client like Linus. He showed up with a friend who wore equally bright clothing and they followed me around asking some very unusual questions. When shopping for brownstones people normally ask, "How wide is it?" and "How close is it to the park?" People in New York City have a deep love of wide brownstones that are close to a park. Linus's concerns were different. He didn't care if he could fit two bedrooms on the north wall with legal light and air. He asked random questions: "Wait. What street is this?" like they had no idea where they were. Followed by "Is this house near a bridge?" like they might need to make a quick getaway. When they said they wanted to see the basement, I thought, *Right, the basement is where they will initiate their new cult members in a ceremony that probably involves drinking Kool-Aid.* I led them down the narrow staircase anyway. I stood awkwardly near the furnace, my eyes scanning for anything that could be a weapon while they looked around. I was relieved when Linus said, "This is dirty and gross," and went back upstairs.

As Linus was leaving I told him to see *Carrie: The Musical*, an amazing off-Broadway show I had just seen. Linus called two days later. He told me two things: One, he loved *Carrie*. Two, he wanted to offer the asking price for my Park Slope townhouse.

I emailed him to ask for some proof of funds to verify his assets and justify the offer to my seller. His response was: "Pls Google if that's ok" in the subject line. Oh. Okay. I typed his name into my search engine. Links to some very attractive clothes at places like Saks and Bloomingdale's popped up—whoa, a purple velvet shirt? There were also pictures of Linus in all his bizarre glory standing next to socialites and models. Serhant, you fool, Linus's family owns the company that makes the amazing purple velvet shirts. Had I googled Linus earlier, I would have learned that his family owned a very successful and well-known European fashion house. What if I had showed him houses based on how he looked? Linus had just moved to New York to run their U.S. operation, and had never been to Brooklyn before. That's why he was asking weird questions. He was also worth about $1 billion, and he couldn't care less what people thought of how he dressed. Linus went from being a cult leader to a personal hero.

Since I sold him that property in 2012, Linus has tossed many other balls my way in the form of referrals, and he's now considered a friend. His weirdness is actually quirkiness, and it's really grown on me. And he hasn't tried to recruit me into a cult even once! When I chatted with Linus at an open house, I never imagined he'd be the source of so many referrals, or my man-date to so many plays. Emilia and I have shared important moments with him, like his baby's first birthday party. That's the amazing thing about sales—just about anyone in the entire world is a potential client and friend. Anyone walking down the street is a big ball of possibility—whether they look like it or not. I have sold multimillion-dollar apartments to people in crazy tracksuits and tiny grandmothers wearing cardigans with holes at the elbows. It's not always easy to determine who really has money to spend, so be open and respectful to everyone to avoid making a big mistake.

ZERO FEAR:
HOW TO TRANSFORM PEOPLE INTO CLIENTS

I have sold apartments to people I've met at the gym and standing in line at Starbucks, finance guys, animal lovers, alleged criminals, doctors, hoarders, grandmothers, artists, college kids, and a family that I asked to "please pass the dumplings" at lunch in Shanghai. Every person on the street is a potential client. Everyone you encounter throughout your day represents a potential sale. That's awesome, right? But, let's be honest, it's mainly awesome if you're the kind of person who has zero fear when it comes to talking to people. Salespeople have to find our own ways to connect with potential customers.

When I started my career, I was renting and selling apartments in one of the most densely populated cities in the country, and I had no clue how to transform any of the millions of people around me into clients. I once asked a pregnant woman at Starbucks "Are you looking for more space?" She wasn't, but she laughed. I had made a genuine connection with her. I didn't come off as some weirdo who harasses pregnant women about upgrading to bigger apartments while they're just trying to get a decaf cappuccino. I was sincere, open, and funny. I said the same thing to another pregnant woman a couple of days later, and I found her a two-bedroom.

Serhant Secret #6

People don't like being sold, but they love shopping
with friends.

Sales isn't about delivering a cheesy line, but about finding
a sincere way to connect with people. If you want customers to
spend their money with you, you must make them feel comfortable in your ability to get them what they want. People don't
like being sold, but they love shopping with friends—this is a
slogan my team hears from me all the time. Think about something a person has done for you—a favor, a loan—it's often not
a stranger doing it for you. It's someone you have a relationship
with. I meet so many people who don't build relationships or
network because they want immediate gratification. Never meet
someone to benefit you today, meet people who can benefit your
future.

Early in my career, two Israeli guys in my office were selling a lot of real estate, and I asked them where they found clients. Unlike Ben Kennedy, they answered. "The synagogue." Oh,
good idea, I thought. But I'm not Jewish, and I didn't feel like
going to church. However, the one thing I did do religiously was
work out.

I had made a deal with a local gym on the Upper East Side
to pass out fliers on the street corner in exchange for free workouts. By now I was a full-fledged, dues-paying member, and the
fancy Equinox in SoHo was going to be my synagogue. SoHo

was a market I desperately wanted to sell in, and I started meeting people the moment I put my mind to it. "Need some water? My name's Ryan." "Need a spot?" "Nice Nikes!" These would be strange things to say to someone on the street. But at the gym, these were my client pickup lines, and they worked. They worked so well that I became addicted to meeting people. The first week I picked up a $3.5 million loft and sold it in four days. The 6 percent commission I made paid for 100 years of Equinox. Literally. And these were just my afternoon clients.

I was ready for more, so why not work out in the mornings, too? I joined the Trinity Boxing Club in the financial district, where mostly finance guys worked out. I hated boxing but it was a good place for exercise and business. Right away I met Frank from Citibank. We hit it off and I sold his condo on Water Street before the end of the month. But I still had my evenings! My third membership was at New York Sports Club. They have 150 locations all over the city and are convenient for slipping in a quick evening workout. If I had an appointment on the Upper West Side, I would swing by their location on West 73rd Street with the mission of coming out with a new UWS friend. Between my three gym memberships I was covering nearly every demographic of New York City, during every part of the day (and bonus, I was more fit than ever).

I made many connections at the gym, but I was deliberate about how I did it. I wouldn't walk up to someone on the treadmill, gesture for them to take off their headphones, and say, "Hi, I'm a real estate broker. Here's my card in case you want to buy or sell an apartment." That's weird and annoying—especially if the person handing you the business card is out of breath and dripping with sweat.

Serhant Secret #7

Connection first, product second.

Never start off by talking about the product. Always make a connection first. If you went on a blind date and the first words out of your mouth were, "Do you want to have sex?" things probably wouldn't go your way. You might even get a drink thrown in your face. Sales is surprisingly similar: You have to be sincere when meeting a potential customer for the first time. Give them a genuine compliment or ask a question to get a conversation started. Get a yes and a smile.

Once that connection is made, you can ease into talking about your product. If you're shy or an introvert, think about approaching new customers as you would a potential new friend. At one time your best friend was a total stranger to you. At some point you met, made a connection, and now you know her deep dark secrets. Like she drinks five pumpkin-Oreo-spice-gingerbread frappuccinos every day.

The point is, I went to the gym to work out—not to just stand around baiting clients. People are attracted to other people with similar likes. Other realtors in New York were connected to potential clients through their religion, kids' school, etc. I had gyms. That was my thing, and I milked it like a protein shake. What's your thing?

Find your happy place and a place you feel comfortable about frequenting often where you can meet new people. I also frequent vitamin shops and the Nike store in SoHo, where I wander around fantasizing about one day having a room just to display a massive sneaker collection. I roam around fellow sneaker enthusiasts and say things like, "Grape was a great color choice for those Air Jordan 1 Retros you're wearing." There was a time when just the thought of talking to a stranger would have given me heart palpitations. Now it's just a simple compliment that could lead to a connection, a new client, or not.

If you want to be really productive, give yourself a quota. Meet at least three new people every day, and get their contact info. Start with just one if you need to, but get in the habit of making friends everywhere you go. A salesperson's network of contacts is her currency. If we equate meeting people to money, meeting three people a day for a year is like depositing an additional 1,095 people dollars that you wouldn't otherwise have!

Serhant Secret #8

Social currency matters. The more people you meet,
the more business you'll do.

It's remarkable when a simple introduction or a passing conversation turns into an unexpected sale or, even better, a long-term client. I've sold apartments to people I've met on the subway and in the bathroom. A connection can be made anywhere. Emilia and I spent our honeymoon in New Zealand, a place we'd always wanted to go. We were staying at The Lodge at Kauri Cliffs, a small and gorgeous hotel, located roughly 9,000 miles from our apartment in SoHo. In other words, we were as far away from potential New York buyers and sellers as possible.

At breakfast one day, a person walked up to me and said what I swear sounded like "Care levitator." New Zealanders speak English with a Kiwi accent. I thought this was a unique colloquialism, so I responded, "Care levitator!" It turned out this was Mr. Fang Von Tonnenberg* and his wife, Brunhilda, of the Upper East Side of Manhattan. They were fans of *Million Dollar Listing New York*, notably the episode in season two when I was selling a $20 million penthouse in Chelsea with—wait for it—a car elevator. We had a quick chat, exchanged contact information, and went on with our vacations.

Fast-forward a few weeks, when we're all back in New York City. I send an email to remind them about our random encounter in New Zealand. Brunhilda responds and mentions their two children are about to graduate from college, and they'll need a place to live. Oh, really? I make plans to show Brunhilda some apartments, and after looking at several they settle on a $4 million two-bedroom in West SoHo that will happily house both kids. This sale wouldn't have happened if I hadn't forced myself to turn away from my delicious Belgian waffle and say hello to a stranger on my honeymoon, and then engage with them. Every single encounter and connection matters.

Just take a minute to think about your day. Where do you encounter other people who share a common interest? What's your happy place? Where would it feel natural for you to initiate a quick conversation? It can be anywhere—the park, a coffee

---

* You already know that's not his real name, but FYI, his real name is much, much crazier.

shop, yoga, etc. Start with something simple like, "Oh, are those almond cookies? I've been meaning to try those. How are they?" That's all you need to do. You don't need to make plans to see a movie or agree to walk their dog while they're on vacation. Start with a simple connection and let it slowly develop into something bigger.

In a million years, I could never have imagined I would meet over a hundred people in a week on average. I was not born with people-meeting muscles; I built them up over time. When weight training, you don't show up the first day and pick up the heaviest weight. You work with the one that's right for you, and as your body gets stronger you increase the weight. It's the same with meeting people. Maybe you'll start off meeting one new person per day. That will get easier, and you'll add a second person, no problem—and then a third. All of this practice will soon translate into more meaningful connections and lead to more sales because people don't want to be sold; they want to go shopping with friends.

THE PERFECT BALANCE

Who grows up dreaming about a career in sales? No one. We all have a story about why we went into sales. You might have fallen into it like I did—just to pay rent—and then you got addicted to the limitless possibilities. You might be the most successful salesperson on your team who wants to sell even more, or you're the new guy who is struggling to get started. You might not be a salesperson at all but want to improve your sales skills in whatever field or business you are in. Whatever your story is and wherever you are in your career, we all have one thing in common: We want to sell more things to more people. We want as many balls in the air as possible, right?

Most salespeople are either too pushy and aggressive, and only focused on the sale. Or they're too accommodating—robotic, and say yes to whatever the client asks. Both of these scenarios prevent deals from closing. To be an effective closer, you have to maintain a connection but focus on the deal first.

The Used Car Salesman Scenario

Consider the used car salesman—stereotypically, he is portrayed as a fast-talking, super slick guy in a cheap polyester suit. This guy isn't listening to anything. He's not taking any time to make a connection with the client. He's all about pushing a product, regardless of whether it's what the client really wants or needs. He doesn't care if you came in for a minivan, he's going to sell you a Corvette. It's way over your budget, and doesn't fit your lifestyle at all—you can't drive a stick shift and there's not enough room in the backseat for your three kids.

Two things can happen here: One, the client is scared away and doesn't buy anything. Two, the client is convinced to buy the Corvette and drives it off the lot—but soon curses the salesman's name when she grinds the gears because she doesn't know how to drive a stick shift, and little Bobby, who has no room in the backseat, is kicking her. Neither of those scenarios make for a happy client, or a repeat sale.

As I started to close more deals, I saw that when I made a genuine connection with clients I was able to show how my product fit into their lifestyles—and not vice versa. If my client loved golf, I'd point out how much fun it would be to live near the driving range at Chelsea Piers. Making that personal connection between product and client is key, and it lays the groundwork for a transaction. It's the difference between closing or losing a sale.

If the car salesman had taken the time to understand the client, she'd refer all her friends to him and invite him over for a barbecue. Unfortunately, this warm and fuzzy scenario rarely happens because most salespeople put on their sales hat, turn up the pressure, and try for the instant close. They work for the sale—and they fail.

We all love big commissions and lofty deals, but sometimes directing a customer to a less expensive option is better in the long run. You don't make repeat customers by pushing them toward a product that's out of their price range. It's always better to do a smaller deal than no deal. Happy customers come back and buy more.

Serhant Secret #9

Don't always sell the most expensive product.

The Tour Guide Scenario

While the car salesman mistakenly worked for the sale and forgot about the customer's needs, another big issue some salespeople have, especially in my business, is that they act like tour guides. "This is a hallway. This is a bathroom. This is a wall. We're walking. We're walking." That's not selling. That doesn't sell anything. Is it nicer than the car salesman approach? Sure, but to sell, the mission is not to be nicer than the next guy. Real estate brokers can't just turn a key, open a door, flip on a light switch, and expect someone to make the purchase. But we say things like, "I don't understand why I can't sell that apartment. I show it all the time!" Oh, do you? You show apartments?

You turn the lights on and everything? Well, that's not selling. Let's go back to the used car scenario for a second. Replace your stereotypical toupee-wearing salesperson with a salesperson who acts like a tour guide. You'd get something like this: "Here is a car. It has four doors, seats six, it's green, it's two years old, etc., etc., etc." Are you inspired to buy that car?

No matter what you sell, spouting facts and pointing to various components of a product is not going to be the thing that inspires a customer to open their wallets and buy. You must use your knowledge and expertise to connect a customer with the product that is the best fit for them. Steve Jobs said it best: "People don't know what they want until you show it to them." Linus wanted an apartment in Murray Hill, but I sold him a townhouse in Park Slope. This didn't happen because I just told him where it was, when it was built, and what the square footage was; based on what I knew about Linus I believed it was the best choice for him—and that he would love it.

Closing a deal is about tapping into emotions. The sooner you can learn to take off the "salesman's hat" and get in tune with your client's emotions and desires, the better you'll become at working the deal. If you're not sure how to do that, remember what makes an exceptional salesperson: a salesperson who works for The Deal.

THE SERHANT WAY OF WORKING THE DEAL

Often, when someone on my team is feeling stuck and just can't move a sale forward, it's because they aren't focusing on the deal. It's incredibly easy to get caught up in the complications, drama, and emotions that go along with selling. Shifting your focus back to the deal will remind you that you have one job: to close a sale for a happy customer, who will then come back and buy from you for *the rest of their lives*. When you work for the deal:

- You Are Relentless: Relentlessly positive, ready, and quick. Your work is your passion and this is evident through every interaction you have with clients.
- You Have Empathy: Your ego will not help you close a deal, but having empathy will. Buying something is an emotional experience. Don't be afraid to put yourself in their shoes—it might be the very thing that helps you close the sale.
- You Are Patient: Be impatient for results, but always be patient with your clients.
- You Listen: You don't just reply, you respond. Learn to let your customers talk first. Listen and carefully comprehend what they're saying before giving a thoughtful response.
- You Bring Value: You use your knowledge and expertise about your product to help connect a customer with what they want.

- You Have Respect: For your customer, your product, and the process. You are honest and authentic in all your actions.

You cannot sell without making a deal. Whether your client pays full price or negotiates, a deal must be made. You cannot push someone into a deal, and you can't expect them to walk right into one either. This does not mean that you're not letting them lead or make the rules (unless you're selling to someone like Mr. X; then just go along with it). You're using the power of assurance to help them feel comfortable enough with the financial and emotional decision they're about to make. Do I guide clients toward one decision over another? Possibly. Do I push a little when someone is nervous about making a decision? Of course. When I sell someone an apartment they love, it's because I listened carefully to their wants, needs, and concerns, and I am able to assure them that they're making the right choice. I always make a point of keeping my eye on the target, and my bulls-eye is always a closed deal.

THE WOW MOMENT

One of my best sales secrets, dubbed The Wow Moment, was something I learned from a shoe salesman at Barneys. It was two years into my sales career and my income had started shaping up. I was finally able to upgrade the Allen Edmonds my dad had bought me because they actually had holes in them. Apparently having holes in your shoes wasn't edgy—it was stupid. I went to

Barneys, an upscale department store, and told the salesperson I was looking to spend about $250, thinking that was an insane amount of money for a pair of shoes. He pointed to a pair of shiny blue shoes that had a distinctive urban-elderly look but were in my price range. Unless I wanted old-man-pimp shoes, I would need to cough up more money than I was planning to spend.

He led me over to another display—this one had all different styles and price points mixed together. A nice simple shoe could be had for $300. But a shoe that would make people sick with envy would cost way more. I realized that designer shoes and Manhattan real estate had something in common.

"Can I show you something? I know you don't want to spend this much, but these are amazing. You have to try them on," the salesman said. He pulled a shoe out of a beautiful, deep purple box. Again, my favorite color. I slipped it on and my foot instantly fell in love. Imagine if you took a baby bunny and turned it into a Prada loafer (without harming the bunny it in any way whatsoever). The shoes were freakishly comfortable, and they looked awesome. I swear I was walking taller and with more confidence instantly. The shoes were magical.

"So, are you on your feet a lot for your job?" he asked.

"Yeah, man, all the time!" Now I'm justifying the price in my head. He went on about how the quality and design would help prevent knee injury. I actually started thinking, *I'm so glad I came into this store today. These shoes could save me from needing a double knee replacement!*

He had wowed me with the quality and value of the shoes. I was soon convinced these shoes would save my career and my knees. I loved them so much, but I couldn't afford the $800 price tag. I thanked him for wowing my socks off.

"No worries! I wanted you to try them because I just adore them. But how about these?" he said, and handed me a $450 pair of Ferragamos. Two hundred dollars over my budget, but much cheaper than the Pradas, so I felt more comfortable buying them. The extra $200 just meant I had to push myself to rent one more apartment that month.

That day I walked out of the store with new shoes and an understanding of how emotions can be used to drive a sale. Having me put on a shoe that was way out of my price range, but not pressuring me to buy it, created a big Wow Moment, and it achieved a couple of important things.

First, my mind was blown. I couldn't believe the difference between a good shoe and an amazing shoe, and I was able to feel it for myself. This is a great technique for upselling someone if they have more to spend. You can't control how much money is in a client's bank account, but you can control how you present the product to them—and that directly impacts how they feel about it.

I ended up spending more after trying on the better shoe. The Wow Moment also gave me a clear understanding of what products were in my price range. It helped manage my expectations. No one wants to hear, "Well, your budget is small, and therefore the sofas in your price range really aren't that great. That's probably why you hate all of them." The Wow Moment is a kinder way to educate and assure a customer about their purchase.

Serhant Secret #10

You can't negotiate with someone's wallet,
but you can negotiate with their feelings.

I first tried the Wow Moment on my client Amanda, who was looking for a rental on the west side of Manhattan and had a budget of about $3,500. When I show apartments, I like clients to see the full spectrum. Typically, I'd start with the apartments within their price range. Depending on the budget, sometimes those apartments may be described as "the kind you wouldn't want your mother to see." Then I show them a more expensive option for comparison. This time I was going to add a Wow Moment to the apartment hunt.

I took Amanda to see a two-bedroom on 74th and West End Avenue. It was in a doorman building, and had really big rooms with built-in bookcases. It was asking $3,400 per month, but it didn't have a view. She liked it, but I could tell it bothered her that there was nothing to see outside the windows. She needed a place fast and she didn't want to lose it (welcome to New York City). I assured her she wouldn't, but then asked if I could show her a place that would totally wow her. She said yes, and off we went. The WOW apartment was a two-bedroom penthouse with a terrace and open city views for $4,250. When we walked in she almost fell over. She ran to the terrace. "How much *is* this place? I *need* it in my life!" she exclaimed.

I told her, but before she got upset, I said, "Don't worry, I know that's too much for you, and who really needs a terrace? I have this same apartment one floor down, for $3,850 without a terrace. Want to see it?" She signed a lease that night.

Factoring in a Wow Moment makes it easier for your client to make a decision. You're also having fun with them! Once Amanda had seen what she could get at her price point, she felt comfortable pushing her budget enough to take the better apartment (which wasn't nearly as expensive as the WOW apartment).

Amanda met her husband while living in that apartment. She brought him home to see the view, or so she says. I wasn't just making a deal that night, I was making a friend for life. Not too long ago we had dinner to catch up. She was having a baby, and wanted to talk about buying her first apartment. At one point she got up to go to the bathroom, and I noticed her coat. I saw the tag—it was made by Linus's family. I laughed out loud and sent him a text. He responded right away, "So funny. Just thinking about you. I want to buy another house."

THE SERHANT WAY

Salespeople are always making connections—they are ready to talk to people in line at stores, at parties, on the street! Just about anyone in the world is a potential client.

Connections must be genuine and sincere:

- Sales isn't about delivering a line; it's about making meaningful connections.
- Think of talking to new customers as just talking to new friends.

A successful salesperson works for the deal:

- You are not a used car salesman. Used car salesman are aggressive and pushy; they work for the sale.
- You are not a tour guide. Tour guides just point to things; they work for the client.

Salespeople who close deals:

- Are relentless.
- Have empathy.
- Are patient.
- Listen.
- Bring value.
- Have respect.

PRACTICE YOUR CRAFT

A salesperson's body and voice are his tools. This all probably sounds crazy, but if you are having any issues with being open and talking to customers, you should try these exercises. If you're thinking, "I don't want to do these things; I'll feel ridiculous," so what? It *is* ridiculous. Who cares? Especially if you become so loosened up, you sell more than the salesperson next to you. Would that be ridiculous? Or do these exercises at home, when you're alone (like I do). We'll just keep it a little secret between two salespeople.

WARM-UPS TO HELP YOU CONNECT WITH CUSTOMERS

YOUR VOICE

Posture First.

If you want your voice to convey qualities that assure customers they are making the right move, start with your posture. You'll sound best if you are standing up tall and straight. You'll also want to be relaxed—try not to be rigid and stiff. You don't want to look like you've just been thawed out after spending several centuries frozen in a cryogenics facility. Stiff comes off as weird. Good posture means easier breathing, which means sounding better.

Stretch...Your Tongue. I'm Serious.

If you didn't major in theatre in college, you probably haven't stood in a circle with a bunch of other students sticking out your tongues in unison. Doing this is surprisingly helpful when you want to sound clear and powerful when you speak. Stick your tongue out as far as it will go, then point it up and down. Hold your tongue behind your top teeth, and then push it out. Rotate your head in a circle to loosen up your neck muscles. If you had walked into my theatre class, it's possible you would have seen all of us flapping our lips and blowing forcefully out of our mouths. This is also a great way to warm yourself up before speaking. To finish it all off, toss in a big yawn or two. Go for it.

Tongue Twisters.

If you want to speak clearly and confidently, practice tongue twisters. Get used to really moving your mouth and your tongue when you talk. Enunciate! Say the following over and over. It can be surprisingly difficult, but as you practice you'll soon see how your words come across loud and clear.

Here are a few to get you started:

- He threw three balls.
- The great Greek grape growers grow great Greek grapes.
- Unique New York. Unique New York.
- Red leather, yellow leather, red leather, yellow leather.
- This is the sixth zebra snoozing thoroughly.

YOUR FACE

There are few things more jarring than talking to a person who does not react using facial expressions. It's unnatural and weird. Try to be aware of all those tiny facial muscles so that they can be more expressive. Practice scrunching up your face as tightly as you can. Think about scenarios that would cause you to do that, like maybe you've accidentally eaten week-old sushi. Hold that expression for a good 10–15 seconds, then release. Repeat three times. Now stretch your face the other way by making a *Surprise!* face. Imagine the face you would make if your dog suddenly spoke to you. That would be so crazy! Hold that face 10–15 seconds and repeat three times. Nice job.

YOUR PRESENCE

You Are a Sales Animal.

Back when my brothers used to tease me for being Cryin' Ryan, I'd yell back between sobs and sniffles, "I'm not Cryin' Ryan! I'm Ryan the Lion!" The fact that I was crying hysterically did not likely give off the impression that I was much of a lion. However, this was a small, but helpful reminder to myself that I was bigger and bolder than I appeared to be. Now for the weirdest advice possibly ever given in the history of books: transform yourself into an animal. If you need a boost of courage—if you need to have a bigger personality—go bananas with this. Bark like a dog, roar like a lion, roll around on the floor if you need to. Let every inhibition go. You have nothing to lose. At the very least, speaking to a new customer or a potential client will not seem challenging or awkward *at all* once you've allowed yourself to trumpet like an elephant. It's fine, really. I won't tell anyone.

CHAPTER 4

The Master of Follow-up

It was April 7, 2017, and I had sold a $17 million apartment to a client named Sebastian Locke, whom I will refer to as the "International Man of Mystery," just like in those Dos Equis commercials, because he looked exactly like that guy. I showed him just six apartments in one afternoon. He fell in love with one at first sight and bought it on the spot. *Yes!* You're probably thinking, *How did you make such a huge sale in just one day? Was it luck? Did you resort to trickery? Please share how you pulled off this astonishing feat!* It does sound amazing. That's a big sale, and I'm going to tell you exactly how I did it. But the truth is, the sale had really started over five years before, and the card I had up my sleeve was follow-up. Classic, well-executed follow-up.

F-1: THE FOLLOW-UP

Becoming a master of follow-up is one of the most important things a salesperson can do to increase sales. Great follow-up comes in three stages, but let's talk about the first one, which is like a golfer swinging at the ball. It's the first step toward making a sale and you can't get very far without it (the golf ball isn't going to move itself). I don't mean calling your leads incessantly and annoying everyone to the point where they dread seeing your name on their phone or in their inbox. Good follow-up, just like a good golf game, is an art form: It takes practice, grace, and diligence to make the ball go where you want, and eventually in the hole—and it works. Had I not been on my follow-up A game, the International Man of Mystery still would have bought an incredibly expensive apartment, it just wouldn't have been from me. Another broker would have gotten that commission. Ouch. And that would have really sucked because he and I go *wayyy* back.

It all started on Thursday, March 8, 2012. I was excited about going to work every day, but this day was special—I couldn't wait to get to the office. I hadn't been this excited since my dad surprised me and my brother with PlayStation 1 on a random Tuesday after 18 months of relentless begging. The first episode of the first season of *Million Dollar Listing New York* had aired the night before, and this was obviously going to change the entire course of my career, overnight. In anticipation of the awesomeness coming my way, I moved my desk out from a dark corner and next to a bright, sunny window. I was like a seventh grader who had abandoned his Trapper Keeper so he could hang out with the cool kids. I felt like a baller. I expected to walk into the office and find a flurry of activity—the phones would be ringing like crazy, and my assistant, Yolanda, would be like, "Ryan, thank god you're here. The entire city has called—everyone wants you to be their broker."

Instead, I walked in to a completely silent office. I sat down at my desk and turned on my computer—nope, no new emails of importance. A few people reached out to say that they saw some show on Bravo with a guy who looked like me, and I should check it out. Great. The whole day passed painfully slowly. *Million Dollar Listing* was supposed to make the phone ring off the hook, and all I got was a fourth-grade friend on Facebook telling me I looked like some guy on TV.

At 5 p.m., it was time to go to Equinox for my afternoon workout and SoHo client search, and then it happened—the phone rang. It was Mrs. Vivian A. Locke, of Scarsdale, New York. "I saw you on a real estate show last night," she said. "I think it was on HGTV. Anyway, I liked you. You're funny. My husband, Sebastian, and I were thinking of buying an apartment in the city and would love for you to show us some places. Our budget is about $3 million." Yes, this was it! A $3 million buyer just cold-called my office! Amazing! At that point in my career I'd only done a handful of deals over $3 million. I made plans to meet with the Lockes the next day.

The next morning I was standing in front of Starbucks, nervously looking through the crowds on the sidewalk to see if I could pinpoint who my clients were, when a gigantic and very shiny Range Rover pulled up. The back door opened up and out stepped an attractive forty-something woman and a tan man with dark hair and a grey beard. He was wearing the nicest suit I'd ever seen, and sunglasses and a watch to match. Since I didn't have my own car or driver, I asked them if they wanted to get into a taxi or take the train. They laughed and said to hop into the front seat—their driver would take us. I didn't grow up under a rock, but I had never been in a car like that, nor had I ever met someone's personal driver. The car smelled like gold, awesomeness, and leather. My life had just changed. I had entered a new dimension of real estate brokerage, and it smelled good.

That day I showed them several apartments on the Upper East Side. We talked in the car in between showings about what they wanted in their New York home away from home. They were incredibly nice people, but they didn't really agree on what they liked. He wanted huge windows, lots of light, close to Midtown. She wanted cozy, gorgeous finishes, right on Central Park. They really liked a beautiful two-bedroom next to the Frick Collection on East 70th Street but they weren't ready to pull the trigger. They dropped me off at my office, and I went back into the Starbucks and got a chai latte to drown my sorrows.

During the next few weeks I kept following up with updates on different listings. When working with buyers, it's important to keep momentum—once a buyer cools on spending this kind of money, it's very tough to get them motivated again.

Mrs. Locke then decided they were open to looking in different areas—the Upper West Side, SoHo, the West Village, Tribeca, Chelsea...and then the Financial District, and oh, did we check out Gramercy? And wait, how about Brooklyn? We haven't seen every inch of that borough yet! Over the next six months I showed Mrs. Locke apartments in small buildings and high rises—I showed her lofts and townhouses, anything she wanted to see. Sometimes her husband would accompany us, but most of the time he was too busy and it was just Viv and me touring the entirety of the five boroughs for hours at a time. I no longer work like this, by the way. I learned my lesson after working with buyer after buyer who wouldn't actually *buy* anything. Now I qualify buyers, I help them focus, and teach them that purchasing property is a process of elimination, not a shopping spree.

I never let the Lockes go, though. I showed them apartments all over the city for a year. Every time they got close to making an offer, Sebastian would find something objectionable—like there weren't enough windows, the lobby was weird, or the closets were too small for his sexy suit collection. I was beginning to suspect that, for whatever reason, these two were not going to be buying an apartment in New York City in the very near future. Maybe they just liked real estate, or liked watching TV shows about real estate. Oh no, I was their celebrity real estate tour guide!

My business had really started to grow during that time, and I had plenty of other balls in the air. I had signed up a new development on Gramercy Park and I was starting a team, but I did not forget about Mr. and Mrs. Locke. I decided I would follow up every three weeks, religiously, until they bought an apartment or I was dead (tragically young), or I read that they'd perished in a fiery car chase in Monte Carlo. I was going to implement the first F, follow-up, by sending them emails about new developments, listings I thought they would like, and highlights from The Serhant Team newsletter.

A successful salesperson is a conscientious follow-upper. Just because you're ready for your client to buy something doesn't mean they are. But when they are, you want to be right there and ready for them. So, make sure you're doing the appropriate amount of follow-up by breaking down your leads into three categories:

HOT: Hot clients are ready to buy something now. They have a time line set. You are in touch with them every day. You're keeping them posted on any product developments or sales. You are making it clear you are working hard for them.

WARM: Warm clients are *thinking* about buying something. They are buy-curious. You are in touch with them once a week, also keeping them posted on developments and sales.

COLD: Cold clients are not actively looking to buy, but that doesn't mean you don't follow up. You are still in touch with cold clients once or twice a month. When they do decide to buy something, there you are, like magic!

The follow-up party with the International Man of Mystery continued. It had been months and now he just wasn't responding, and neither was my travel buddy Viv. I had follow-up time blocked out in my calendar every week for warm and cold clients. I spoke to hot prospects every day. Following up is not really a fun task, so put it in your calendar so you're forced to do it. Why would I devote an hour to follow-up when I could be watching *Grey's Anatomy*? Because my calendar said so, that's why. Eventually, this will become automatic, like muscle memory, and you won't have to put "follow-up" on your calendar anymore. But until following up becomes as natural to you as brushing your teeth in the morning, follow-up has got to go on the calendar.

International Man of Mystery continued to hear from me every few weeks even though he did not answer any of my emails, but then, suddenly:

Thursday, December 12, 2013
From: Ryan Serhant
Sent: Thursday, December 12, 2013, 1:30 p.m.
To: Sebastian
Subject: 33 East 74th

Dear Sebastian:

Have you heard of the new development at 33 East 74th?
It is six row houses that used to belong to the Whitney
Museum, now being converted to condos.

10 units between 4,000 sf 3 bedrooms up to 10,000 sf
5 bedrooms. Starting at 13M. Expected to be completed by
2015.

Hope you're well. Could work well for you!

Ryan Serhant

From: Sebastian
Sent: Friday, December 13, 2013, 10:56 a.m.
To: Ryan Serhant
Subject: 33 East 74th

Ryan,

Thanks. I had not heard about this. Something to consider.

I hope all is well and best wishes for a merry Christmas
and a happy new year.

He answered! I was almost giddy, like I had just won the lot-
tery. However, the International Man of Mystery did not buy

one of those gorgeous apartments at 33 East 74th. The big $17 million deal was still four years away and over a hundred follow-ups later. If you think I knew he was eventually going to buy, you're wrong. If you're wondering if I ever thought of just giving up, I didn't. Here's the thing: most people would have given up; they would have tossed him to the side like socks at Christmas. Why put in the effort if he isn't going to buy an apartment right now? But following up is so easy. When you incorporate follow-up into your regular sales practice, jotting off a quick and friendly email is practically effortless—and it's free. It's *free*! It costs you nothing to send an email, and it takes less time than it does to make yourself a donut-shop-flavored Keurig coffee. If there was any chance the Lockes were going to buy an apartment—ever—it was going to be from me. Let the follow-up parade continue!

When you follow up with a lead, don't just send a generic email or a note saying, "Hey, do you still want to buy a hot tub? Because I have one I can sell you." Who wants to get that email? Always follow up with value in your message. Include information about a sale, or a new product. You just came across an article that says, "People who have hot tubs are so relaxed that they outlive poor slobs who do not have hot tubs." Include that along with a friendly message about how you're offering free delivery this week only!

I follow all my clients on social media. I also save all of their birthdays in my calendar. The other day I noticed that Greta Lambert's son James had just celebrated his tenth birthday. It was an opportunity for an easy, friendly follow-up message. I shot her an email, "Wow. James is growing up so quickly, your apartment must be feeling small." Greta responded, "Ryan, good to hear from you, it does feel small!" Now she's a warm lead and I'll follow up next week with some listings in her area.

The friendly follow-up has a stronger impact.

Finally, on a Sunday in early December of 2016, I got a call from the International Man of Mystery himself. I hadn't heard from him since that one brief email around Christmas—three years earlier! During this call, I learned a few important things.

1. He was now divorced. *Um, not surprised.*
2. His financial picture had changed. His budget for an apartment had increased from $3 million to between $15 and $20 million. *Oh my God.*
3. He called me because I had "been so diligent about keeping in touch for so long."
4. Follow-up really works, and it is absolutely worth the small amount of time and effort it takes.

We made a date to start looking at apartments, and this time, without Mrs. Locke, he was able to make a decision very quickly. He closed on April 7, 2017. My commission check was $510,000, or about $280 per day since the day I first met him.

F-2: THE FOLLOW-THROUGH

The Harmony House at 61 West 62nd Street is an Upper West Side high-rise close to Lincoln Center and Central Park. While the name of the building conjures up images of sunshine and rainbows, something quite different was waiting behind the door of apartment 21E. The owners were into the Gothic Revival look, and the entire apartment was outfitted to look like a Spanish Catholic church. You know. Normal.

There were frescos and prayer candles everywhere, and as I walked through the apartment I may have imagined hearing organ music. In the living room, right next to the brown velvet sectional sofa was an actual confessional booth from the nineteenth century. The confessional booth was convenient, since it soon became clear this apartment was really meant for sinners. The first time I was in the apartment I noticed a hook hanging from the ceiling in the middle of the living room. And guess what? It wasn't for plants. It was for a sex swing! There was also a surveillance system, and you could watch what was going on in every room of the apartment from...every room of the apartment. Because goth-chic does not say "home sweet home" to most people, this apartment was an incredibly tough sell. Eventually, with the help of underwear models, I was able to perform a miracle and sell the church-of-kinky at full asking price about six months after listing it.

During the time it was on the market, I met a lot of buyers. One, Mr. Campbell Killian, had come to an open house hoping to find more space for his growing family. Instead he found a makeshift church, and that wasn't what he was looking for apparently. Since Campbell appeared to be a normal person, I completely understood why this apartment wasn't a match for him. I added him to my database and proceeded to give him the full Serhant follow-up treatment.

Eventually, I was fortunate enough to have the opportunity to sell Campbell's duplex-penthouse on the Upper West Side. There were many pros to this apartment: it was 2,750 square feet and had three terraces and 600 square feet of outdoor space, high ceilings, four bedrooms, and five bathrooms. This place was ideal for a family. But where there are pros, there are also cons. This place had a big con. Two penthouses had been combined, stitched awkwardly together into a Frankenstein-esque creation. The rooms just didn't fit together right. There were two living rooms, one on each side of the kitchen, and the apartment had more stairways than an Escher drawing.

It was a tough sell. Immediately upon walking into the apartment every single person said, "Weird layout," and exited the apartment via one of the countless miniature sets of stairs. A big pro was that the apartment was kid-friendly with lots of play space, and I ended up having a party for moms and kids. This was the only time I got my face painted, wore clown-sized sunglasses, and danced with toddlers to make a sale. And it worked.

Enter the second F: follow-through. If *follow-up* is hitting the ball, *follow-through* sets the direction of where that ball is going to go. I'm terrible at golf (and baseball, and all other sports with balls), but I still know that if you don't follow through when you swing, that ball is probably going to fall flat or go sideways.

While I was happy to have found a buyer for Campbell's penthouse, I also learned that real estate was a bit of a hobby for him. He enjoyed following trends, researching new developments, and generally staying up-to-date on the market. He is often in touch with me with questions about listings he sees. One time he wanted me to research a house he was curious about—in Iowa. Some realtors might find this annoying, or view it as something they "don't have time to do." Anytime someone on my team tells me they're too busy to answer clients, the next day they're not on the team. Customer service and follow-through are paramount to referral business from clients just like Campbell. So even though I had no idea what houses in Iowa were worth, I was happy to get more information for him. It's worth it to me, because anytime Campbell thinks about real estate, I want him to automatically think two things: (1) Ryan is who I turn to for all matters real estate; and (2) When I ask Ryan to do something, if he says he will, it's done every time.

Serhant Secret #11

Always treat clients like they are brand-new.

Your database of customers isn't a mailing list; it's a list of relationships. If you want to have repeat customers and sell more, you must take care of these relationships—even at times when there isn't immediate money to be made. I tell my team to think of each and every person they work with as a brand-new client, even if they've been clients for years. Always remember that your clients are your social currency. If someone gave you a $100 bill ten years ago, it's still worth $100 today!* An old client is as valuable as a new client!

Anyone can follow up by pushing calls and emails, but follow-through is the next level. It's simple: do what you say you're going to do. If you tell a client you'll do some research and get back to

---

* To those of you who are whipping out your calculators and are about to email me that, due to inflation, that $100 bill isn't really worth $100 today, let me save you the time by assuring you that I'm familiar with the concept of inflation. I'm just trying to make a point!

him, do it. If you say you will answer your emails within twelve hours, do it. If you make a promise to yourself that you're going to meet three new people every day, don't sell yourself short. Do it.

Following through is a huge opportunity to show clients you're invested, that you care about them, and that you're dependable. When you want to sell more and build relationships with repeat clients, follow-through is the simple tactic that can set you apart from everyone else. Want proof? After lots of follow-through, Campbell bought a $36 million apartment on Park Avenue with me.

Be accountable to yourself and others with follow-through. If you've told yourself you're going to devote a certain amount of time to finding new leads and you're having trouble keeping that promise, create accountability. Make a plan with a team member, or create a competition to push you to do it.

F-3: THE FOLLOW-BACK

It was December 2016 in New York. That meant I would spend nearly every evening until the end of the year awkwardly socializing at holiday parties around town. I was at the annual Madison Realty party at the Boom Boom Room above the Standard Hotel. It's a great networking event. I was standing around with a group of people when I met a banker named Jonathan Stern. I introduced myself, quickly moving my teriyaki chicken skewer into my other hand before reaching for a handshake. Stern was developing some properties in Greenpoint, Brooklyn, an area I had really come to appreciate. We talked about how quickly Greenpoint was becoming Brooklyn's hottest neighborhood, and how we loved the area's unusual combination of Polish restaurants and art galleries. We exchanged contact information, and I went to get a drink and explore the mini-hamburger selection before heading home to my favorite human in the world, Emilia. In the elevator ride down to the street, I sent Stern an email telling him I enjoyed meeting him five minutes ago, and I'd love to set up a meeting to see his projects. I asked if Tuesday or Wednesday would be better.

Never wait to follow up. Follow up *now*. It's one of my little tricks to get attention. No one follows up faster than I do. And when you want to set up that follow-up meeting, propose dates that work for you. Don't just ask if they're free—take control of the destiny of your working relationship!

Stern responded that he and his brother-in-law had a development going up on McCarren Park on the Greenpoint side of Brooklyn. Yes! But there was one catch: "I already have a broker working on it," he said. "But would you like a tour of the building?" Yes, I would.

The building tour took place on a day that I would describe as "snowing-sleeting-insane-hellfire-winter." It was just a few weeks after our run-in at the Boom Boom Room, so I bundled up like I was Jon Snow and made my way carefully to Greenpoint. After the tour I thanked everyone, and told them I'd do whatever I could to bring them as many buyers as possible. I added Stern's brother-in-law Chad Gessin to my contact list, and made sure they received The Serhant Team monthly newsletter. I did *not* try to poach the client, because that's gross and that's happened to me and I hate it. I started following back. I would keep in touch, making a point of showing them how diligent I am, and how dedicated I would be on their next project. I wasn't the broker on this project, but I wanted to be in the forefront of Chad's mind if he had a new development going up. This was my opportunity to possibly get the ball back into play.

Fast-forward six months. It's June, and I get a call from Chad out of the blue on a Monday. He says they're about to launch 868 Lorimer, the building we toured back in January, but he needs a new broker. He said I was relentless with my outreach, and that's the kind of broker he needs selling his apartments. "Are you interested?" Of course. Then he asked if I could launch the project by Thursday. Um, sure.

I had no idea how I was going to get everything ready in time. For a new development of this size, I am typically involved for at least six months, and most times a year or two before launching sales. This time I had four days! Four days to get all the visuals, digital and printed marketing collateral, floor plans, written descriptions, ads written and developed, launch party designed and planned, invites created…and the list goes on. We needed a marketing plan, a pitch, and a sales team all ready to go in less than a week. It was crazy, my hair definitely went greyer, but we did it and it was amazing. We sold 90 percent of the units in the building in six months and broke two price records while doing it. All because I sent an email to his relative in an elevator after a holiday party and then followed back with them for months.

Following back is different from just following up with a client you're already working with. Following back is keeping in touch with past clients or people who did not hire you, and it is one of the biggest opportunities that salespeople miss out on.

Following up is touching base that first time. It's hitting the ball. Following through is making sure the ball goes where you want it to go. And following back is getting right back to the ball so you can hit it again! That's how golf works, and that's how sales work. And if you follow the Three F's, as I've shown you, you will get that ball in the hole.

THE THREE F'S

FOLLOW UP   FOLLOW THROUGH   FOLLOW BACK

I can't tell you how many times I've gotten a new client because that person never heard from their broker again after a closing. Ever again. Why? The idea of someone not following back with a customer makes me want to throw up. It's easy, and a sincere way to build a relationship with a repeat customer. It's also a way to keep a door open for an opportunity that isn't yours to be had at the moment. I don't get every job I pitch (very much to my dismay), but I don't see that as the end of the opportunity. I can still show a developer or client how awesome I really am (and why they should hire me next time) by following back.

The closing of the deal is just the beginning of the relationship. It is a huge mistake to assume the relationship with a customer ends when they buy your product. The closing of the deal represents the beginning of a new chapter in the relationship.

Follow back after the sale—ask how they are enjoying that hot tub, if the kitchen renovation is going well, or even if the dress they bought for their daughter's wedding was a hit. Follow-back leads to repeat customers.

Another big developer in New York had a new condominium project I desperately wanted to sell in Park Slope. I pitched my heart out for this project, but the developer didn't go with me— he thought I was too small at the time. I could have just been annoyed or angry. Too small?? Really? Or I could follow back to show that this perceived flaw was ultimately something that didn't matter at all. I decided to send the developer a gift as a thank-you for letting me pitch him. I ordered a 10-foot fig tree that took four people to deliver and had it sent to his office with a note that simply read, "IMPACT." My new development team may have been small at the time, but make no mistake, I know how to make an impact.

He noticed. Two years later, after many follow-ups, he called me and said he had a new project that will be Brooklyn's first super-tall skyscraper. He wanted me to pitch him. I nailed it. At least I thought I did. That is, until he said I would hear back from him in a couple of months. What? I could be dead by then... except I'll be alive because I really want to sell this building.

I could let that drive me bananas and sit around by the phone like a 16-year-old waiting for a girl to call, or I could use this as an opportunity to follow back. My team and I worked together to figure out how we could make another impact, something bigger and more meaningful than a tree. We bought a very attractive, modern, and architecturally interesting bookcase, and had it delivered to his office. But we didn't stop there. The next day, we sent a book with a note. We did the same thing the next day. And the next day. Every. Single. Day. By the time he decides which broker to use, he will have a well-curated collection of books sitting on his beautiful bookshelf. I knew I was the right broker for the project, and I was determined to send him a book a day until he chose me. Did it guarantee it would get me the job? No. It did not. But it would be impossible for him to not think of my team, our passion, our determination, and our generosity every time he walked into his office. And *that* is a big impact.

A month later he sent me an email; the subject was "BROOK-LYN." The body said: "U WIN. LET'S DO IT. BOOKS CAN STOP NOW."

As salespeople, we can't get every single client. Hearing, "No, I've gone with someone else," is just part of our business. It can suck. I hate it sooo much, but that doesn't necessarily have to be the end of the story. Deals can die, but relationships never can. Using the Three F's gives you some control. Following up, following through, and following back provide an extra, free, and easy opportunity to show clients what you're really made of (awesomeness, etc.). The next time you don't get a client you want, just remember this isn't necessarily the end of the chapter. Get out your calendar, block out some time for follow-up, and see where the Three F's can take you. And if all else fails, there's always the fourth F: Fuck it.

THE SERHANT WAY

The Three F's Rule is one of my most valuable sales secrets, and I don't understand why everyone isn't doing it all the time! Block out time in your calendar for follow-up, and watch how new business practically lands in your lap.

THE FOLLOW-UP

1. Never expect people to get in touch with you.
2. Follow up until you get a YES or you read their obituary.
3. Follow up with active clients every. single. day.
4. Follow-up is smacking the ball—it's the first step.

THE FOLLOW-THROUGH

5. Do what you say you're going to do.
6. Create accountability if you need to.
7. Never forget you don't just have clients; you have relationships.
8. Follow-through drives the ball where you want it to go.

THE FOLLOW-BACK

9. Keep in touch with past clients.
10. The relationship does not end at the closing.
11. Touch base with clients you lost.
12. Follow-back is your opportunity to get the ball back into play.

CHAPTER 5

The Seven Stages of ~~Grief~~ Selling

Every salesperson knows this client—no matter what industry you're in. Sarah didn't want an apartment, she wanted a unicorn. The apartment she wanted just didn't exist, and nothing made her happy. I showed her two bedrooms on the Upper West Side (too small), three bedrooms in Long Island City (too big). I showed her apartments on low floors (too low) and then on high floors ("Ryan, I can't live here, I have vertigo!"). But I was determined to find something she liked. It nearly killed me. During what was becoming a very long and drawn-out process, I made sure to pay attention to everything she liked and didn't like. She said yes to new construction, outdoor spaces, and open kitchens—and no to older buildings, low ceilings, and apartments with cats (the cat goes, but the kitty litter smell remains). She really liked an apartment on 23rd Street. Unfortunately, during the showing we could hear the residents on the other side of the living room wall having sex, and whoever lived on the other side of the master bedroom was an avid video game player. A listing on the Upper East Side had a great terrace. But as we took in the view and she was about to make an offer, the guy next door climbed over his terrace, right onto the one we were standing on to say hello. True story.

Eventually, I found a new listing that ticked off Every. Single. Box. No cats, sexy video gamers, or terrace hoppers. It had the right number of bedrooms, there was an outdoor space with a view, it was the penthouse but it wasn't too high up, and it had an open kitchen. We walked in, and instead of thanking me for being the best broker in the world because I had found her a unicorn with magic glitter rainbow wings, she took a quick look and said, "No. I don't feel it."

She didn't feel it? I started to think I wasn't going to find Sarah an apartment, at least not before I hit retirement age. I hated the idea of giving up, but I couldn't find her anything she liked. The following week I asked Sarah to meet me for a drink at a bar in Midtown because I had to cut ties with her or start taking blood pressure medication. When I got to the bar we ordered our drinks, and I was getting ready to initiate a really awkward conversation when she suddenly said, "Hey, did you know there's a really good strip club right across the street? Let's go!" It turns out that Sarah loves strip clubs. Really loves them. Sarah had a very successful career in the fitness industry. She was a workout fanatic and could probably do more push-ups than I could. Apparently, she appreciated an opportunity to check out other women's bodies. So, off to the strip club we went!

Sarah was entranced by the display of washboard abs and well-cut biceps. To be clear, this wasn't a freaky sex thing. Sarah was like a professor doing research—curious and appreciative of the level of core strength it would take to perform an aerial invert on a pole. I never had the chance to break up with her because we were too busy pondering how many grams of lean protein these women ate daily. I learned something about Sarah that night. I realized that watching these young women was like a release, perhaps it was even an escape from her own insecurities. She was older now, a mom, and recently divorced. Even though she was fit, Sarah told me she lamented the fact that she no longer had the body of a 21-year-old stripper. It's like the strip club empowered her and gave her an extra boost of motivation. We left at midnight and Sarah went home to work out.

I still planned to give Sarah some space, but the next day I noticed a listing in Chelsea that seemed too good to be true. The price was low, because the building was surrounded by new construction and they were having trouble selling. It had a good view, an outdoor space, and a great gym. But the kicker? It was next to a strip club. I knew if this didn't work that nothing would, and I would have exhausted every possible option. It would be time to retire this ball.

I gave Sarah an address and asked her to meet me there. I told her I had something to show her, and she should prepare to be wowed. She had a big smile on her face when I arrived, "Ryan, I thought you were showing me an apartment. If you wanted to hang out at Scores why didn't you just say so?" She looked a little confused when I led her through a doorway right next to the strip club. We got into the elevator and went up to the penthouse on the 12th floor, not high enough to give her vertigo. It was a beautiful apartment—big rooms with a bright, open kitchen. Even better, it had a private rooftop cabana with an outdoor kitchen. While the interior space wasn't as big as she would have liked, she was happy with all the positives, including the proximity to Scores. She made an offer that day; she had found her perfect home.

Serhant Secret #12

Checking boxes is for to-do lists,
not for getting deals done.

When Sarah said no to the initial apartment with the view that I thought was perfect for her, I wanted to jump right off the balcony I had worked so hard to find. It ticked off the boxes, but she didn't "feel it." Checking boxes doesn't get deals done. Good salespeople know what to expect from clients during every phase of the deal, because they are in tune with their clients' emotions as they pass through each phase. Sarah was nervous about her apartment search, and kept hoping there would be something better. This wasn't just a decision about an apartment—it was about her future. I realized these were the same feelings she tapped into at the strip club. I wasn't struggling to find Sarah an apartment because she was difficult, but because she was disappointed—she had hit that stage in the sale. When I was able to empathize with what she was feeling, I was able to guide her to the right place and get a deal. When we found her a perfect home—one that made Sarah feel comfortable to make such a big purchase—she was able to commit. There's often an underlying element that moves a person into a comfort zone of buying.

I had a client who insisted on living downtown, wouldn't venture above 23rd Street for anything…except the opera. When an apartment came up that sounded ideal for her at Lincoln Plaza, I was convinced the proximity to the opera would be the bonus element that would make her fall in love. She was reluctant, but when I showed her the apartment and guided her over to the window, I saw her eyes light up. There was a view of Lincoln Center's famous fountain—she could practically hear the music from the opera house right in her living room. This was the moment when everything clicked together. Of course, she bought it.

Ultimately, in every sale there's always the same emotional cycle, which ranges from excitement and disappointment to happiness and relief. To manage a lot of balls you must be ready to handle every part of the cycle, and know which stage each ball is in. It's like a brewing storm that you must be prepared for. Tornados don't just pop out of nowhere. There are usually warning signs. Rain, high winds, flying cows. This is true whether someone is buying a wedding dress or a pair of skis. Good salespeople learn to anticipate what direction a deal will go, and they understand how each stage of the sale will help them get deals done faster. The goal is to emerge from the messiest of sales, even as ruinous as an F5 (aka the Hand of God tornado), unscathed.

THE STAGES OF EVERY SALE

As a real estate broker, I've seen it all. Nothing surprises me anymore, ever. Except that one time when a client gave me an adorable baby pig as a gift—I did not see that coming. But every sale I make runs through the same seven stages. There is nothing new. Shopping, whether it's for a home or for a pair of shoes, is more about mastering the seven stages of ~~grief~~ selling than a need.* Sure, we all need shoes and a place to live. Humans require shelter, and I don't know about where you live, but the streets of New York City are disgusting and I'd rather die than touch them with my bare feet. But if shopping for a home or a pair of shoes or a massage—or anything at all, really—were only about need, it would never take more than a couple of minutes to purchase anything. The thing is, no one ever walks into a shoe store barefoot. Chances are most people own at least one pair of shoes, and, technically, you only need one pair to protect your feet from freezing cold temperatures and sharp, rusty nails! People walk into a shoe store because buying more shoes fulfills a want. The emotional process of buying a product, any product, is the same with every transaction. Some transactions are just quicker than others. Some jump around the chart a little. But 95 percent of the time, every deal follows the same stages of ~~grief~~ selling I'm going to outline for you below. If you learn to anticipate what customers will likely do during each stage of the sale, you'll be in a great position to use the appropriate tool to anticipate your next move, and keep the sale moving toward a close.

Stage One: Excitement

Remember Campbell Killian from the Master of Follow-up chapter? I sold his combined penthouse with the weird layout after I had a party in it for babies. Well, later on, I had the good fortune to help him buy his dream home, and he had a budget of $20 million (OMG).

---

* I resort to shoe-buying examples frequently, as I am a very experienced shoe shopper.

Campbell was smitten when he saw the apartment. This was it! It was in a beautiful building on Park Avenue with 15-foot ceilings. He could imagine making pancakes for his kids in the gourmet kitchen, or watching the sunset over the city on his gigantic terrace while drinking phenomenally expensive scotch. Campbell. Was. Pumped. Then he heard the price. The asking price was $40 million. This apartment was my WOW stop. I told him there was a similar apartment on a lower floor with lower ceilings for less. But Campbell had seen the light and there was no going back, even if he was spending more than he planned. We offered $30 million but settled at $36. Back to being pumped!

- In the excitement stage a buyer is focusing on all the positives of the product—and how it will change their lives for the better. They are falling in love.
- Signs you're in the excitement stage include: comments such as "I love this," "Oh my God, I'm so happy I'm getting this," "This is the greatest day of my life." Fist pumps. Tears of joy.

Stage Two: Frustration

Enter complications. The contract was difficult to negotiate. The seller was really tough and fought back on every concession Campbell wanted. Did I mention the building wasn't even built yet? It adds to the frustration when the product (apartment, car, custom-made sofa) doesn't actually exist yet. Campbell was starting to feel this apartment wasn't worth all the trouble. Uh-oh. The tornado alarm has sounded.

- In the frustration stage the buyer is focused on the negatives; they are suddenly seeing everything that is wrong with the product. They haven't pulled out of the deal, but they're annoyed. This phase could also be called the blame phase, since most buyers start to blame other people (most often that's us) for their frustration.
- Signs you're in the frustration stage include: impatient phone calls and texts, emails asking why things are taking so long, threats to back out of the deal.

Stage Three: Fear

Campbell's frustration blossomed into full-fledged fear when the seller refused to contractually agree to what the decibel level would be in the apartment that was not yet built. He worried he was overpaying. If the seller was being difficult about decibel levels, he must be hiding something! He feared the super-high ceilings weren't high enough. Ultimately, he questioned whether he was making a bad investment. Campbell convinced himself there was an equally amazing apartment just waiting to be found, so he killed the deal. Though it had been love at first sight, he decided to walk away from his dream apartment with its cozy pancake breakfasts and stunning sunsets. We started the process over and started looking at more apartments. Fear had touched down like a tornado and was destroying everything in its wake.

An interesting development: in this case, fear actually revived the deal! It soon became clear that Campbell just couldn't love any other apartments the way he loved the Park Avenue apartment.

His fear morphed from "I can't commit to this" to "Ryan, what have I done?? I've made a horrible mistake! Can you help me win her back?" You know how what goes up must come down? In sales it's the opposite: what is down (prices, deals, a client's emotional state) must go back up. Only once a client has entered the fear stage are they emotionally ready to climb back up the ladder of positivity and make a deal. Out of all the fear comes a positive result.

- In the fear stage the buyer starts to feel afraid of what he's taken on. "Can I handle this?" "Did I spend too much?" "Do I really need this?" They are actively questioning their decision to make the purchase.
- Signs you're in the fear stage include: angry, incessant phone calls and texts; emails in the middle of the night featuring multiple exclamation points; swearing; yelling; more tears—but now the sad and angry kind.

Stage Four: Disappointment

Good news, the apartment was still available! The seller was still open to doing the deal, and even agreed to some vague language regarding the sound levels in the apartment. They made it official; they signed a contract. But before a bottle of champagne could be uncorked, disappointment reared its very ugly and incredibly annoying head. The minute the paperwork was signed, Campbell worried again that he had spent too much. How did he go $16 million over his budget? He told his bank not to send the wire for the down payment. He was disappointed and "had to think." Ugh! Stage four is the worst.

- In the disappointment stage, the magnitude of the purchase starts to weigh on the buyer. They start to seem overwhelmed, anxious, and distant.
- Signs you're in the disappointment stage include: the client feeling regret and remorse, forgetting that this apartment/car/wedding gown, etc., was the one that made them feel all tingly inside, ignoring your texts and emails.

Stage Five: Acceptance

Campbell came to terms with what he knew from the beginning: this was his apartment, and no other could match it. He made the deposit, and he needed to move forward. His wife thought the apartment was light-years beyond even her wildest dreams, and this made him happy. Back to visions of pancakes and cocktails. I also reminded him of how hard we fought for the best deal. He was now both calm and pumped. Stage five is a pretty good place to be.

- In the acceptance stage the positives start to flow back. The buyer starts to remember the journey they've gone through to procure this amazing item! The fear melts away and the joy slides back.
- Signs you're in the acceptance phase include: happy spouses and children in for pop-up office visits, thank-you notes or gifts, peace, quiet, and calm.

Stage Six: Happiness

The more Campbell thought about his totally insane new apartment, the more excited he got about the idea of moving in. The next chapter of his life will begin in his dream home. He's like a little kid awaiting his birthday—crossing off days on the calendar. He can't wait for the big moment.

- In the happiness stage the customer is bursting with excitement. The joy is on par with the last day of school, Christmas morning, or the day your mom says, "Fine, you can get a puppy."
- Signs you're in the acceptance phase include: constant emails about when the product will arrive. They connect you to their friends who they think should buy from you. The happiness phase is the best time to ask for referrals.

Stage Seven: Relief

Shortly after Campbell closed on his apartment, someone bought the one directly above his for $45 million—$9 million more than he paid. Markets come and go, but Campbell felt relieved that he bought his dream home when he did. The time was right.

- In the relief stage, the customer is now comfortable with the purchase. Any obstacles faced, all the highs and lows no longer matter. The purchase was also their idea the whole time! Imagine that.

- Signs you're in the relief stage include: bragging, boasting, "It's such a good thing I bought that when I did," "I can't believe that guy paid even more than me! What a sucker!"

THE SERHANT TOOL KIT OF EMOTIONS

We all know that sales are usually bumpy. I will always do everything in my power to close a deal, but there are times when there is nothing I can do to save it. It's DOA (dead on arrival); I have to let it go. Most sales are messy but I've created a toolbox to help. It's full of different techniques I use to smooth over difficult situations and gently guide clients through the stages of the sale. There is no one single solution for each problem a salesperson will face because every sale is different. But I've learned that these tools can be effective in many different situations: When a client is being difficult or is MIA, maybe they're in the frustration stage. Nine out of ten times, if a client is bursting with excitement about a purchase, be ready to tackle the fear phase because it's right around the corner and will be arriving soon. If you find yourself in a situation where you need to guide your client to a different place, use these tools:

"We've All Been There."

When I'm working on a particularly tough deal, where the sale is full of drama so gut-wrenching my client deserves to be nominated for a Tony, I remind myself to be empathetic.

I'm a salesperson, but that doesn't mean I'm immune to the stages of the sale. None of us are. It can help to remember that we've all been there. We've all wanted to buy something and have ended up riding a roller coaster of emotions. When I started selling more apartments, I decided I deserved a nice watch—every successful person who bought an apartment from me wore a great watch. My boss went with me to the watch store on Madison Avenue, where I proceeded to go through every stage of the sale, just like my clients! Finally I saw it, a nice shiny Breitling. "Oh, hello, beautiful watch!" Then I saw the price. I was like, "What is wrong with you, Boss? Why would you bring me here? These prices are crazy." But "I looovvvveeee it." Only to be followed by, "Wait. This city is probably full of beautiful watches. I must see them all!" But "I love this one!" Finally, I bought it, then promptly felt sick that I had spent all that money. Surely I could have gotten a better deal. But then I put it on, and it looked fantastic! Thank God I bought it! I could be walking around town wearing a Swatch! Who would hire that guy to sell his apartment? I went through every single stage of the sale in a span of 30 minutes. Buying something is an emotional experience, so remember this when you are in the messy middle of a tough sale. Put yourself in your clients' shoes. Talk to them. Listen to them. Try saying:

- "We've all been there."
- "I sympathize with what you're going through."
- "I understand how hard these decisions can be."
- "This is the hard part, it's going to get easier."

"We Are in This Together."

I love selling brownstones, but these deals can be delicate. If I'm not extra attentive, these deals can die a quick and violent death via an inspector or an attorney. It is an inspector's job to find problems—and there is just no such thing as a problem-free brownstone. Most of them are really old! If I know an inspection is about to take place, I'll talk to the buyer about what they should expect. I assure them that when the inspector comes back with a gloom and doom story about a seven-year-old furnace, there's no reason to panic. If I didn't do this, they would kill the deal the second they heard words like "lead paint." I assure clients that we can address these issues in the contract, and that there's no need to flee the city for a nice split-level ranch somewhere in the Midwest.

To keep things running smoothly throughout every stage of the sale, I'm as upfront as possible, and I set expectations. I'm preparing the customer for possible outcomes, and assuring them that we will tackle these challenges together. It's almost like a doctor-patient relationship. Sure, your doctor is probably a genius—but that's not what makes you feel good about her ability to help you if you break all your toes in a freak bowling accident. It's her knowledge. You're confident she'll fix your toes. She's assured you she's up to the task, and you're in it together until you hobble out of the hospital on crutches. When times get tough in any kind of sale, you need to have a doctor-patient–level relationship. Your clients need to know they can turn to you for help, and you'll be with them until the problem is solved. Try saying:

- We are in this together.
- I will be with you until this is finished.

- I'm here for you throughout this entire process.
- If there's a problem, we'll figure it out together, one step at a time.

THE INDECISIVE CLIENT:
PUSH, PULL, AND PERSIST

Some people would rather exist in a dark, murky state of limbo than make a decision. Decision making is often hard and uncomfortable. It's much easier to just sit on your couch binge-watching *Black Mirror* than it is to take action. If you are in sales, inaction is enemy number one. There is nothing more worrisome to a salesperson than indecision. It can stall or even kill a deal. To combat this mortal enemy, I use a combination of push, pull, and persistence to guide clients to the next stage of the sale.

The Push

Barking orders at clients is a good way to freak them out and get them to either buy from someone else or simply avoid you. While we can't dictate what a client should do, we can Push. We can ease them off their ultra-comfy sofa of indecision. The Push is gentle but firm, and it can be just the thing that gets the client unstuck and ready to make a purchase. Ways to use the Push include:

- *Offer Incentives:* While I certainly don't want to be viewed as "Ryan Serhant, discount broker," I have made deliberate decisions to lower my commission to get a listing I wanted or to get a deal done. Think about what else you can offer a client to get them to take action today. Is the awesome suit they are hesitating to buy going on sale tomorrow? Tell them about the sale, and that you'll speak with your manager about getting them the sale price today. Sometimes adding a small incentive is just the thing that will tip a customer to yes. Offer two for one. Offer free shipping. Small incentives create more sales, and I'd much rather make $10 than no dollars.

- *Create Urgency:* We all know that people tend to want things they can't have. Is the handbag they're looking at the last one in stock? Create urgency by sharing that nugget of information. Obviously, you need to know what kind of urgency you can reasonably create. If a guy is trying on a sweater that he's picked up out of a pile of a hundred, he clearly knows it's not the last one. Create urgency a different way. Maybe say, "Are you going out tonight? That looks great on you! You should wear it!"

The Pull

The Pull is what it sounds like: pulling an item away from a client to prompt them to move forward. It can be very effective if done right. To execute the Pull, you must use grace; it's not like ripping off a Band-Aid. I often use the Pull when selling very, very expensive apartments. There are moments when a client is hesitating and I have to say, "This is really expensive. It might be too expensive for you. Let's look at less expensive options."

This move results in an instant "gut-check"—it's like hitting the RESET button on a frozen iPhone. The gut-check causes the client to realize that, yes, this is what they want, and, yes, they can afford it.

The Pull isn't just for expensive items. It's also a great tool to use when you know a product is wrong for a customer. That's when, you, the salesperson get to come in and save the day! "Oh, you're interested in buying a chinchilla for your kid's birthday? Have you considered a guinea pig? They are considered the best first pet for children because they are so friendly and easy to care for!" When that parent realizes she made the better choice, and it's all because you pulled her away from the chinchilla, she'll come back to you when her other child wants a pet rattlesnake.

Persist

In some cases, neither the Push nor the Pull is quite right. In these instances, a salesperson needs to Persist. You're not actively pushing, and you're not pulling back, but you are reminding them that the product they are considering is perfect for them. Recently, I had a client who was $100,000 away from closing a deal for an apartment on the Upper West Side. He refused to move up if the seller wouldn't come down. I knew that the apartment was actually priced right! To have come down from the asking price would have been underselling it, and I knew that. I persisted with my client. Every two days I sent him a message about the deal. One message would be about how I'm trying to hold it for him. Another message would be about a new comp sale that justified the asking price. A third message would be my suggesting he see it again. He agreed to take another look. We talked about his issues and it was clear he was in the fear stage. I used my tools to get what was down back up and he bought it for $9 million.*

THE ELEMENT OF SURPRISE

The element of surprise can give you the upper hand when guiding a client through the stages of the sale. To be clear, I'm not talking about throwing a party or dressing up in a clown suit and popping out from a behind a bush yelling "Surprise!" That would be terrifying, and scaring a customer to death is a terrible idea. When my team uses surprise, we're incorporating an unexpected element into the process to help move things along. We do this by how we present information or manage expectations. There are many situations where a salesperson has to present unpleasant information. In my world that usually means a buyer has backed out of a deal. When this happens, I will milk every resource I have to find a new buyer ASAP. This means I can call up a client and say, "The bad news is that your buyer backed out because he decided to join a competitive curling team in Moscow. *But!* The good news is I got you another offer!" The bad news is instantly replaced by the good news. For people who sell other things, this could mean that a product won't be ready on time or an order was placed incorrectly. Instead of calling up your customer and dropping the bad news, take time to think about what little

---

* Only in New York City will a $9 million deal fall apart over essentially 1 percent. That's insane, but it's important to remember here that this isn't ultimately about the money; it is always about the emotions.

surprise you can add to remedy the situation and maintain the relationship. "I'm so sorry that your order won't be received on time. Please know that I've reduced my commission to make this a better deal for you, you get free shipping, and 20 percent off your next order." Sometimes surprise comes in the simple form of exceeded expectations. Sales is customer service—never forget that! There are countless ways to show clients that you value your relationship. Surprise clients with your tenacity, persistence, empathy, and hard work. My team goes above and beyond in this department.

"Ryan. You need to call Jackson Hitchcock. Now. He's in full-fledged stage three (Fear). You must save him! Then you need to email Casey Monroe; she's in stage four (Disappointment)—but I'm anticipating a quick recovery and she should be up to stage five (Acceptance) in no time. But you'll need to check in with her." My assistant, Jordan, is like a triage nurse. He knows the signs of each stage and can detect if a client is slipping from stage two into the dreaded stage three. He knows which case is the most dire and requires my immediate attention. Knowing where my clients are in the process emotionally is invaluable to me. I'm not jumping on a phone call blindly; Jordan has prepared me for what I'm about to face so I can be ready to handle the situation with the most appropriate tool. Knowing that Jackson Hitchcock has reached the fear stage of the sale, I can think about what I can say or do to reassure him and get him safely across the finish line to a done deal and a champagne toast in his new apartment. If Casey Monroe has hit disappointment, I can raise her spirits by sharing the news that the exact same apartment she just bought one floor higher has sold for $300,000 more than hers. Toss her that little element of surprise and she's well on her way to feeling relieved that she got such a great deal. If I didn't pay attention to my client's emotional needs, a great big pile of sad and lonely balls would inevitably come crashing down, and it would be hard to get them back in the air. These are deals that would have been done if I had been doing my job correctly. Learning to recognize these crucial stages that exist in nearly every sale can help you keep your balls in play.

THE SERHANT WAY

Understanding and learning to identify the seven stages of the sale will not only help you close deals faster, but it will make your life much easier.

1. Excitement: Wow, I love this. I'd better get ready because my life is about to change.
2. Frustration: Wait! I can't control every part of this; who can I take out my frustrations on? I know! The guy who is selling me this suit, car, refrigerator, or engagement ring!
3. Fear: What if I find something better? What if there is a better deal to be had? Is this the best thing for me?
4. Disappointment: I did it. I spent all that money. I know I could have done better.
5. Acceptance: Well, hell. I did it. Life is short.
6. Happiness: Actually, this is going to be awesome! I'm happy about this.
7. Relief: I'm so glad that's over! It was definitely the right thing to do!

THE SERHANT TOOL KIT OF EMOTIONS

Empathy: "We've all been there." Put yourself in their shoes.
Assurance: "We are in this together." Reassurance that you are in it until the end.

The Three P's

- Push: Gentle prodding
- Pull: Gentle taking away
- Persist: Consistent reminders that this is the best product.

The Element of Surprise

- How can you present the information in the best light? Make a positive sandwich. Stick the negative between two pieces of positive. Sure, the negative is the real meat of the sandwich, but you can't get to it without biting into the delicious positives first.
- What actions can you take to surprise clients with your dedication?

CHAPTER 6

You Need to Get FKD

Remember Mr. X? To refresh your memory from a few chapters ago, I flew to Paris to meet with him and I was either going to sell him my first multimillion-dollar apartment, or wake up in a bathtub minus one kidney. You'll recall that story ended happily. *Eventually.* After a lot of drama and what felt like years of back-and-forth, I made my first really big sale—and I got to keep all my internal organs! I felt unstoppable. Once this deal went through I couldn't wait to slide headfirst into my rightful role as a star real estate broker. Except no one was responding to my ads, calls, or the postcards I sent out. I wasn't having any luck with new clients I met on the street. I wasn't able to close a single deal. What was happening?? Doesn't everyone understand I flew to Paris and played drinking games late into the night to get a contract signed? *That's dedication.* But after selling Mr. X his apartment I entered a Very. Long. Dry spell. The next four months were scary and disappointing. Why wasn't this working? Was I not as great a broker as I thought I was? Maybe that one deal wasn't the career-maker I thought it was, and instead it was just a fluke. An outlier. A random and crazy transaction that never should have happened in the first place. Every unreturned phone call sparked a new wave of self-doubt.

I had an opportunity to get out of the city for a while. I went on a trip to Mexico with my family. My spirits lifted as soon as I saw the beach. I spent the day swimming and lying in the sun. If my career was over, I might as well enjoy the glorious beaches before I moved to Colorado to spend the rest of my life prodding cows on a ranch. But the sun is a sneaky bitch and I have a terrible habit of underestimating its power. Later at dinner, my sister looked at me and said, "Um, are you okay?" *Oh my god, can she tell I haven't sold anything in four months just by looking at me?*

"Ryan, what's up with your face?" Huh? Now that she mentioned it, my face was feeling kind of, um, tingly. By the main course, my face had erupted in blisters and felt like it was frozen shut. I was sunburned so badly I had to stay in my hotel room watching telenovelas, cloaked behind a dark curtain and a thick layer of 2.5% Mexican hydrocortisone cream. After three days, I decided to brave the outdoors and go to the movies. I'm watching *Mr. Popper's Penguins* dubbed over in Spanish, glad I can't understand any of Jim Carrey's jokes because my face would not be able to withstand the pain of laughter, when I get an email on my phone.

> Hi, my name is Maximus. I have a postcard here from 2009 I've saved for a while. Are you still a broker? I have an apartment I want to sell on the 69th floor of the Park Imperial on West 56th. It faces Central Park. Call me back please.

Dios mío! I would have smiled from ear to ear if it wouldn't have made my face bleed. Is this for real? The Park Imperial was a mythic building. I had heard tales of its magical, sparkling, and ultra-expensive apartments. This was a great opportunity, and the timing was awesome. I was excited, sure—but then I remembered my face. Until literally a few minutes ago, I was back in that place I vowed I'd never be in again—worrying about how much longer I could afford rent in New York City before I had to move home. I remembered how excited I felt after closing on Mr. X's apartment just a few months before. I had gotten a taste of how amazing a sales career could be—and I wanted more—but nothing happened. I got lucky when Mr. X had randomly emailed me, and now I had an awesome opportunity because a guy saved a postcard I sent out two years ago. But did I want to be the broker who waited around for things to get dropped into his lap? At this rate, I'd sell one or two homes a year—maybe. That wasn't good enough. Why was I waiting for people to come to me? Why wasn't I creating my own opportunities? As I took a final lick of a mango-chili–flavored Mexican lollipop, I realized that I felt empty inside. And I recognized that feeling. It was the broke, scared, lonely feeling I had that day on the subway. Except now, it was a little different. What if that emptiness was just my body and mind's way of telling me I had room for more? Maybe that emptiness was really hunger. I was hungry for more deals and bigger successes. I decided the moment I walked out of that Mexican movie theatre, with a large sombrero shielding my blistered, tomato-red face from the sun, that I was done waiting for random luck. I needed to redefine my entire approach to my career as a salesperson. Outlier deals like the one from Mr. X or Maximus who waited two years to call would be considered a bonus from now on. I was going to take charge, and move forward. And that meant I was going to have as many balls in the air as I could. Each ball would represent a single sale, a possibility, an opportunity to expand and grow. I just had to structure my days in a way I never had before. I was ready for the big time— and that meant figuring out a way to keep everything accessible and in order so I could have lots of balls in play. This was going to be fun.

TIME STEALER VERSUS TIME MANAGER: HOW TO MANAGE YOUR WORKLOAD

There are countless books and workshops on how to be a successful salesperson. What frustrates me is that none of these books discusses exactly what a salesperson can do with their day and their time to improve sales and productivity. A lot of the advice includes clichés like "Be happy! Follow your passion and you'll never work a day in your life!" How is that advice helpful in any way? Time is our only asset as salespeople. There are only so many hours in the day to work with as many clients as possible, so how do we maximize our waking hours to sell more?

Growing up in a disciplined household, where there were rules and structure, gave me a big advantage when it came to time management. I've learned that most people who say they are busy sooo aren't busy. They are stressed out, overwhelmed, and not managing their time properly—so they announce, "I'm busy." La di da. People aren't busy—they are bad time managers. Unless you are a cardiac surgeon who is in the middle of reattaching the right ventricle of someone's grandfather's heart—you're not really that busy. You can probably take a call or answer a text (the cardiac surgeon, probably not). You are doing yourself a huge disservice if you don't manage your time properly. If you're not careful, your poor time management will also impact other people, because when you don't do your job right, you often have to drag other people in to fix things. And you know what that makes you? A *time stealer.* Time is a bitch, and it moves very, very fast. If you are a salesperson who has ever thought, "Oh my god—I have so much to do, what should I do? When should I do it—but whoa, the day is already over and I'm in bed again!" then listen carefully, because this chapter is going to help you take back your time. You can do more with your day than you think you can. I promise.

RYAN'S DAY

I probably do more in the early hours of the morning before most people have poured their first cup of coffee. My day actually starts the night before in my brain. It usually goes something like this:

11:00 p.m.: Email is cleaned up, calendar is set. Wait, there's another email! Answer it! Check on deals. Kiss sleeping wife. Plug in phone. Close eyes. Ready, set, sle....

4:30 a.m.: Did I go to bed? Yes, I did. Get up. Pee. Check pulse. I'm alive!

4:33 a.m.: Read *Daily Mail. NY Post.* You know, the important stuff.

5:04 a.m.: Make oatmeal. Drink water.

5:05 a.m.: Wait on microwave.

5:06 a.m.: Oh my God, it's still so early.

5:08 a.m.: Actually eat oatmeal.

5:15 a.m.: Check email. Respond to emails that came in overnight so that people know I'm up before them and ready to DOMINATE.

5:30 a.m.: Go to gym.

6:00 a.m.: Gym selfie. Post on Instagram.

7:00 a.m.: Shower. Shave (face or legs, or both).

7:29 a.m.: Kiss Emilia goodbye. Grab her inappropriately as I'm running out the door.

7:30 a.m.: Get in car with Yuriy. Ready, set, GO! Off to office or first appointment.

8:00 a.m.: My "Finder hour" in the office.

Serhant Secret #13

Your morning should always start the night before.
Wake up knowing exactly what your day entails
and what challenges you are facing.

I am hardly the first person to believe that getting up early improves productivity and increases profits. It's unlikely that Tim Cook gets out of bed around 11 a.m. and shows up at Apple around noon. The earlier you get up, the more time you have to conquer the world. This is not news. But there's another reason I drag myself out of bed and march myself over to the gym before the sun comes up. It means the hardest part of my day is over by 6:30 a.m. Physically, I've survived the pain that is a 300-pound dead lift superset with a 300-meter ski-erg sprint, and even though my mind was trying to tell me there was no way I could do more burpees—I prevailed! While I never know what challenges the day will throw my way, I know that if I managed to do 500 sit-ups, I can certainly handle a buyer who is freaking out, or a seller who is screaming at me on the phone because it's my fault no one likes his *Star Wars*–themed kitchen.

What's the hardest thing you have to do? Stop reading and do it now.

It's human nature to want to ease into your day—wake up when you're ready, drink coffee, listen to a podcast, pick out an outfit, or stop at Starbucks for a vanilla latte before you decide how to tackle your day. Often it's not until you get to work that you realize, *Oh, I have to have a really difficult conversation*, or *I have to call Barb about her order.* But then you have a meeting, and another meeting—and when that's over, you decide to answer all your emails. *Call Barb* is running through your head like a playlist on repeat. And you ignore it. Your day gets more hectic, and, oops, you never made that phone call. Now you're at home and, instead of being relaxed, you're stressed and anxious. You toss and turn all night and wake up feeling terrible and still dreading that phone call.

In Serhant's world, this scenario would have gone down like this: The night before, you'd think about what the following day will look like. Realize, *Oh, I have to call Barb. That will be hard! I'll deal with it first thing in the morning. I have an 8:30 meeting, so I'll go in 15 minutes early so it's handled.* Get to the office with your latte, make difficult phone call, discover it wasn't as bad as you thought, and move on with your day without a nagging voice telling you to call Barb. Go home at night sans any anxiety and actually enjoy your life. Waiting to deal with a complicated situation just prolongs your anxiety and can make things worse by breaking down the relationship further. Dealing with it right away also adds a hint of surprise. The message you're sending is, "I'm not avoiding this challenge at all; in fact, I'm so on top of it!" The person you are calling will be surprised, too, and they may even be caught off guard by your prompt attention to the situation because *no one* else does this.

My schedule is packed with appointments and calls every half hour—there are balls flying all over the place. Some of the balls I'm working with are about what you'd expect. I have people who are counting on me to sell their apartments. I'm in constant communication with them, giving them updates on open houses and incoming offers. Then I'm showing apartments to people who want to buy them. I'm keeping them posted on any new listings. I'm taking pitch meetings with developers so that my business is always expanding, and I have a team of 60 agents who need to be able to reach me. My other balls are a little atypical and might include: a photo shoot with me and 15 dogs on a bed to show that one of the buildings I'm selling is super dog-friendly. Riding an eco-friendly electric bike around Brooklyn to promote my listing. And traveling to rural Pennsylvania to chop down a tree with a cabinetmaker for an episode of *Sell It Like Serhant*. If that sounds chaotic to you, it's because it is. We've all heard the saying, "from chaos comes order." I see it differently: from chaos comes sales.

Serhant Secret #14

Don't be afraid to push yourself to take on more. If you're
the one who creates the chaos, then you can control
the chaos.

I know that every single thing I do today has an impact on
tomorrow. It's all about setting a bigger foundation, so that I will
sell more, get new clients, and land more deals. I'm not happy
unless I go to bed happily exhausted. There are the same 24
hours in my day as there are in yours. I put in the work and stay
focused. And I've learned that the key to success is to break down
your day into three distinct categories.

THE FINDER, KEEPER, DOER METHOD

I'm not interested in making *one single* sale, even if it's gigantic.
If you're thinking of your business or work as selling one thing,
then this is probably not the book for you. One sale is a job,
SELLING is a career. If you want to have an insanely successful career selling, you need to have a lot of balls in the air, at
all times. A lot of potential sales means a lot of balls—the more
balls, the more sales, the more success.

When I got back from Mexico and my face had returned to
normal, I understood that I needed to do much more than I was
doing to grow my business. What could I do differently to be successful? Especially since my entire company was just me? I realized

I needed to wear three distinctly different hats to grow my business. I couldn't just toss on a baseball cap that said "Boss" and expect my business to undergo a mythical transformation. Being the boss or CEO wasn't enough—success required financial planning and work. That's when I began dividing my work day into three sections: the Finder, the Keeper, and the Doer. This was a watershed moment for me as a businessperson. Was this what Thomas Edison felt like when he finally got his fucking lightbulb to work? Probably.

The Finder

When you're wearing your Finder hat (it's a strictly metaphorical hat), you're working to create new business. You're taking pitches, working a sphere of influence, and making decisions about how to steer the business forward. The Finder thinks about the business as a whole movement. The Finder must expand the company's rolodex.

The Keeper

When you're wearing your Keeper hat, you are focused on the financial profile of your business. The Keeper is in charge of economic forecasting, paying taxes, strategizing on how to complete tasks efficiently, creating budgets—and making decisions about how much the company will spend on advertising and marketing, etc. When you want to set goals for yourself, your team, or your business, reach for your Keeper hat. The Keeper understands that those goals must be realistic, and needs to know what must happen in order to reach them. The Keeper also budgets time—because time is currency for salespeople. How much time should you devote to pitching a new client or pitching a product that isn't moving?

The Doer

The Doer carefully executes all the work that the Finder has brought in, and the Keeper has strategized and budgeted for. The Doer leads the business to victory. For my team, the Doer sets up appointments, handles showings, runs open houses, and processes applications and contracts. The Doer's work is the day-to-day work that needs to happen for you to be successful.

Going back to the office after my trip to Mexico with the Finder, Keeper, Doer method jotted down on the back of an airplane barf bag helped my head feel like it was attached to my shoulders once again. I didn't have a crystal-clear plan about what I was going to do, but I felt like I had taken an important step as an entrepreneur. I wasn't waking up lost anymore. I now had a game plan for my day, literally mapped out in my calendar in three separate groups. I got to my office excited about putting my Finder hat on. That meant I was gung-ho on finding new business as the Finder of my company. It meant that I needed to take steps to create relationships and locate new developments, because the Finder specializes in the art of expansion. Forever. If the Finder doesn't do that, the Keeper has no projects to manage and no money to budget or spend, and the Doer won't have any work to actually *do*. It all trickles down from the Finder. I was mostly still doing rentals at the time, so I decided I would create relationships with some landlords. I cold-called them to introduce myself as someone who would do a great job renting out their apartments. Fueled by my new role as the Finder, I also cold-called some For Sale by Owner ads, even though it was as terrifying as that time I asked Liz Jose to the prom.

In my first week as the Finder I managed to get an appointment with a couple selling an apartment at 401 East 60th Street. The apartment had been decorated by Madonna's interior designer—and everything inside it was turquoise. When they asked me what properties I had sold previously, I had to confess that I had no experience. Yet. I convinced them to let me run their open house. The deal was if someone bought it while I was there, they'd pay me a commission, and if someone bought it any other time during the week they owed me nothing. If you think I sold this all-turquoise apartment in my very first week, I'm afraid you are incorrect. They ended up hiring a broker with 20 years of experience. It didn't matter. I still felt good about myself. I had put on my Finder hat and reached out for business in a calculated and structured way, something I had never done before. I had little money but had made deliberate choices about how much money and time I would spend on the turquoise apartment. With my Keeper hat on, I decided that I could afford to spend $200 on advertising and taxis. And I could dedicate about 10 hours each week showing the apartment. This helped ensure that if I sold it I would make a good profit.

Before developing my Finder, Keeper, Doer method, I had just worked in Doer mode, only thinking like a Finder here and there and definitely never thinking like a Keeper. These three stages of work are going to look different depending on where you are in your career. If you're in the early stages, most of your day will be spent doing Doer work, like I did. That's fine! But you must still block out time for Finder and Keeper work. Maybe you get in to work an hour earlier than everyone else, or use your lunchtime, or force yourself to stay awake after you put the kids to bed. It doesn't matter when you do it! But you need to devote Finder time to creating relationships and steering your career forward, and Keeper time to making decisions about your financial profile if you want to sell more than anyone else! As you increase your sales, the amount of time you spent doing Finder, Keeper, and Doer work will shift. This is what getting FKD might look like for you:

FINDER, KEEPER, DOER
"FKD"

FINDER	KEEPER	DOER
PROCURE CLIENT	STRATEGIZE FOR CLIENT	DO THE WORK

Finder Work

Do anything you can to find relationships—from talking to people on the street, to cold-calling, to going to three different gyms. Make a vow to meet potential clients every single day.

Give yourself a specific number, and get their contact information!

Later on, as you start to establish relationships, you can use current relationships to cultivate new ones. Let your clients know how much you appreciate referrals. Referrals from people you've worked with in the past are *the best*. Also leverage successes you've had into new projects. For example, once my team started to sell out entire buildings, we were able to leverage that success into getting more buildings to sell.

Keeper Work

It doesn't matter how much money you have to work with. You must immediately start making decisions about finances if you want your business to grow. How much will you spend on marketing? What are your goals? How will you meet those goals? I had very little money to work with in the beginning. For every paycheck I received I saved 50 percent for taxes (as sure as death), 40 percent for rent and food, and the remaining 10 percent went back into the business. I used that 10 percent to make postcards or maybe place one ad. Find a scenario that works for you, but always make sure you're investing back into the business. As business starts to pick up, you can strategize about other ways to use the money. Should you be buying gifts for clients or taking them to dinner? Depending on your ultimate goal, as you grow bigger you'll need to make decisions on a larger scale. Today I budget for my team, and I'm making decisions about advertising costs, marketing materials, staging, team outings, and lead generation.

HOW TO SET GOALS
YOU WILL ACTUALLY REACH

Setting goals is crucial to your success, and it's an important part of your Keeper work. Reaching those goals? Even better! I've learned, though, that most salespeople do not set themselves up for success when setting goals. I love big goals! But not unless they are accompanied by a realistic plan to help you get there. I can't tell you how many times I've met with new team members to set goals and had them excitedly say, "I'm going to *make* a million dollars this year!" My response: "That's great! How will you do that?" Then we start to break down the numbers and look at how many apartments they will have to sell, and at which price point, to make that goal. Suddenly they are feeling less excited, and that's the opposite of what a goal should do. Goals should inspire you! When you set a goal for yourself—say, earning $100,000 in a year—break down exactly how much you'd have to sell in order to reach that number. Be honest, is it reasonable? If it's not, scale back, nail your goal, and plan to move the needle even further next year.

Doer Work

Doer work can be everything and anything. Turning on lights, sending emails, answering the phones, opening mail, placing ads, licking stamps, putting postcards in mailboxes—whatever work has to be done to get the deal made. I did everything from ordering Twizzlers in bulk to showing apartments, to painting apartments, staging apartments, and measuring apartments to make sure a couch would fit, and taking out the garbage when a seller forgot to. For you it might mean paperwork and contracts—whatever work it takes to support the deal. If you are just starting out, the bulk of your day will be filled with Doer work and that's fine! As you grow, you will spread into the Finder and Keeper mode, but chances are there will always be a bit of Doer work in your life. Eventually, you may have an amazing team who takes care of the Doer work. Now that my days of ordering Twizzlers are behind me (mostly), I am able to focus on creating pitches, negotiating, maintaining contact with developers, managing my team and admins—and writing a book.

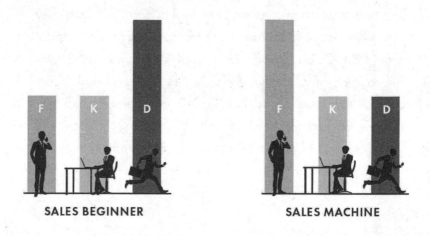

LET ME SAVE YOUR SANITY

I wore all three hats for a long time. While today I wear my Finder hat more than when I first entered the sales business, I certainly pop on the Keeper hat and the Doer hat every day, but for much less time. My Doer work has transitioned from bugging a landlord for keys to a 5th-floor walk-up in the East Village, to sitting down with a developer and an architect to plan what types of apartments we will build in a 200,000-square-foot condo building. How many one-bedrooms, two-bedrooms, and three-bedrooms will the building have? But just because your career is in the full-on three-hat-wearing stage doesn't mean you can't outsource some of your work. Human beings cannot be in more than one place at a time (I wish this were not the case). When I was doing rentals, it wasn't unusual to have several appointments for showings at the same time. If I could clone myself, I could do three showings at once and potentially triple my income! But I majored in theatre and knew nothing at all about somatic cell nuclear transfer, so I'd ask another broker in my office to help out. Instead of losing a client because I was too busy, I had other brokers do the showings I couldn't do myself, and I would give them half the commission. I learned early on that it's much better to make 50 percent of something than 100 percent of nothing. Don't be afraid to outsource or share the work to leverage yourself. You can't do everything. Do you work on a retail floor? Divide the store in half with a coworker and share customers. That's called a zone defense in football, and it is highly effective.

Serhant Secret #15

Catch half a ball before you let it hit the floor.

Another way to use leverage is to create your own mini-team. When I shot the first pilot episode of *Sell It Like Serhant*, I worked with Marc, who was struggling to sell golf equipment in New York City. His coworker was selling way above her quota every day. One of the challenges Marc faced is that he'd have to fight for customers with the other salespeople. If Marc and his coworker teamed up instead, they could combine their strengths to dominate and make more money.

Sales is the best job in the world, and it's also really, really hard. Working in sales is like riding a roller coaster—every day. Blindfolded. You don't always know when you're about to hit a big curve or plummet over a drop. I know what sales-induced craziness feels like. It's overwhelming, and easy to feel lost and insecure—and there's no drug to fix this. I honed in on my FKD system out of total desperation. I needed to save my sanity, and routine and structure was the solution.

Early on, like many of you, I didn't have a boss. No one was telling me what to do or when to do it. Creating a work system for myself kept me from quitting and going to some boring job, and I haven't felt overwhelmed or like jumping off a bridge since I started using FKD. I don't want you to feel that way, either—there's too much at stake, namely, your sanity and your career. I want you to wake up ready to jump up and attack the day, and to feel that you only have to do one thing: you have to get FKD.

THE ULTIMATE SALES MACHINE'S SCHEDULE

Ultimately, how you choose to structure your day and when you choose to schedule your Finder, Keeper, and Doer time is up to you. I'm not your boss! But if you are anything like me, you just want someone to tell you what to do to increase success and when to do it. Here is a suggested schedule to follow:

4:30 a.m.: Wake-up time. Check emails and answer them. People will wake up and see you mean business.*

4:45 a.m.: Healthy breakfast. I like oatmeal, but do *you*?

5:15 a.m.: Exercise. You need your body to work!

6:30 a.m.: Read newspapers, look for articles that are relevant to what you do.

6:45 a.m.: Shower, get dressed, look awesome.

7:30 a.m.: Manage spouses, kids—packed lunches? Homework? Goodbye!

8:00 a.m.: Arrive at office, and DO YOUR HARDEST THING.

8:30 a.m.: Do your finder work. How can you expand your rolodex today?

* As you know I'm a fan of getting up early. If you absolutely, cannot get up that early, adjust the schedule above to suit your wake-up time. But, really, would you just consider getting up earlier?

9:30 a.m.: Check out your schedule for the day. How much time do you have for keeper work, doer work, and follow-up?

9:45 a.m.: Team meeting: Talk to a team member about working together on a project to create leverage.

10:30 a.m.: Follow-up: Call your hot and warm leads.

11:30 a.m.: Follow-back: Send an email to that client you lost, checking in to see how things are going and informing them about the new products you have.

11:45 a.m.: Keeper hour: Decide how much money you have to spend on marketing for your next project.

12:30 p.m.: Lunch with potential client.

1:45 p.m.: Follow-through: Get client that information they asked for during lunch.

2:00 p.m.: Doer work: selling, selling, selling.

5:00 p.m.: Follow back with that person you just met at Starbucks. Email them right away!

5:15 p.m.: Doer work: Brainstorm about marketing materials.

6:15 p.m.: LIFE: Hello family, dog, girlfriend, children. How was your day?

11:00 p.m.: Quick email check. Answer emails to show people how you dominate!

THE SERHANT WAY

In this chapter, I've just given you the secret sauce to my success. If you want your business to thrive, you must carve out time for FKD every single day, no matter where you are in your career. The Balls Up theory is the key to volume sales. To the countless people who have asked me how I manage my time, I can't wait to hear about how your sales increase once you get FKD.

GET FKD

The Finder

The Finder is the CEO who makes decisions about how to steer the business forward.

The Keeper

The Keeper is the CFO who makes decisions about the financial profile of the business.

The Doer

The Doer is like a soldier—carefully executing all the work that leads the business to victory.

PRACTICE YOUR CRAFT

As you've learned by now, I say "ready, set, GO!" all the time. It's something my dad used to say to motivate my brother and me to get moving when we were kids and it has stuck with me ever since. Now when I say "ready, set, GO!" it's like I'm sending a special signal to my brain—it's not just about the words, it's what they mean to me. Saying "ready, set, GO!" is my starting ritual.

The moment I utter those three simple words I'm cueing myself to focus, take initiative, be awesome, work hard, and DOMINATE. I'm not necessarily superstitious, I don't think everything I've built would come crashing down if I forgot to say "ready, set, GO!," but, to be honest, something would feel off. Those words center me and that's why I make a point of starting each day with this easy ritual. Consider creating your own ritual and working it into your morning to get off to the right start:

DESIGN YOUR OWN STARTING RITUAL

- Is there a phrase or even just a word that's extra meaningful to you?
- Is there a goal you're working hard to reach? How can a starting ritual help you reach that goal?
- It can be anything that works for you—it's your ritual, and all that matters is that it inspires you.
- Commit to incorporating this ritual into your morning. Do you notice a difference? If so, I want to know! Email me at ryan@ryanserhant.com

CHAPTER 7

The Four Tenets of Work

On October 29, 2012, Hurricane Sandy hit the East Coast. A lot of people around New York and New Jersey lost their homes and cars, and many lost their lives. There was massive flooding, there were mandatory evacuations, and most of the city was shut down. Manhattan doesn't run well without things like electricity and running water. It was like the city that never sleeps had been knocked unconscious—and it was *spooky*. I was lucky to be safe and unharmed. The biggest problems Sandy gave me were existing in complete darkness for a few days, having to walk up 14 flights to my apartment because the elevator was out of order, and, if I wanted to make a call, I'd have to walk about 20 blocks uptown to where my phone could actually get service.

Compared to many people, I got off easy, but that didn't stop my parents from worrying about me. After my power went back on and life got back to normal, they came down for a visit to see how I was doing. I had been working a lot, even during the hurricane, and the grind of it all was getting to me. We were in my living room, and I was complaining to my dad about how much it sucked to wake up at 5 a.m. while most of my friends slept until 7 a.m., and how hard it was being in sales—no salary, no regular paycheck, no benefits, no guarantees of really anything at all. Maybe I should have gone back to school and gotten a MBA. Why didn't I do that?! I also wanted weekends off again. I'm not sure what I was hoping to achieve by complaining. Maybe I wanted my parents to know how hard I was working, and it's possible I wanted a bit of sympathy or a good pep talk. That's not *quite* what I got.

My dad cut me off and said, "Stop right there. Do you think that I ever *wanted* to wake up early and go to work every day? No. I *wanted* to sleep in. I *wanted* to hang out. But that wasn't the job." Mind. Blown. As long as I could remember, my father was up every morning at exactly 5:50 a.m. He woke up and got out of bed without an alarm clock. It's like he knew instinctively when it was time to rise—kind of like a vampire. Getting up at that ridiculous hour was hardwired into his very being. My dad didn't mess around and because he wouldn't use an alarm, hitting the snooze button wasn't even an option. He showered, shaved, grabbed a piece of toast, and was off to start his day. And, yes, I was under the impression that was *exactly* what he wanted to be doing—working long hours, all the time. My father is the most disciplined person I know. He was military-like when it came to work. All those years he had been getting up before dawn and hadn't ever complained about it? Not even one single time? I will never forget that moment. Everything was put into perspective for me. It was like Superman and I were having a drink and he confessed, "Ryan, here's the thing. Flying actually makes me feel pretty sick, and it's exhausting helping people all the time. Take last week, for example. This kid was trapped under a truck so I had to pick it up to save him. It was really heavy and now my shoulder is *killing* me. Hey, do you have any ibuprofen?

But, well, you know, that's the job!" What my dad said to me reinforced that everything we do is a choice. It was my choice to get up early and to work harder. I was complaining about something that *I* had decided to do. And if *I* didn't consciously decide to choose hard work, a different choice might be made for me. I wouldn't sell anything and I'd be broke again. But, more importantly, why was I making the choice to get up so early and work on weekends? Because, in the end, I desperately wanted to succeed.

WORK FOR YOUR CAREER, NOT THE JOB

Growing up, we always lived in areas surrounded by trees—our neighbors could have been aliens, but we'd never have known because we couldn't see them. With all the trees, there was never a lack of sticks that needed to be cleared from the lawn. My brother and I had been earning money for our diligent stick collecting since the first grade. As we got older, stick collecting transitioned into weed whacking and lawn mowing. In high school, I spent my summers working for Testa Building and Remodeling in North Andover, Massachusetts, as a contractor's laborer, aka a grunt. My job included demolition, which meant hauling incredibly heavy loads of debris to a dumpster in the scorching heat. Lots of people redo their roofs in the summertime. I would carry 80-pound bags of shingles up the ladder, with the skin on my shoulders slowly being flayed off by the weight of it. It was hard work. It was exhausting. And I can remember every single dollar I made those summers. By the time I went to college, my parents had moved to Colorado, and I spent my summers working as a ranch hand. Roof shingles and kitchen debris in the suburbs of Boston were replaced with bucking broncos and cow shit on a 2,400-acre ranch in the mountains. The open skies and sheer beauty of it all made up for the fact that manual labor is not fun. I'd drive the length of Trout Creek, feeding the fish in the stream, so that the people who came for fishing expeditions would actually be able to catch live trout. I'd move the horses and cattle around and mow the various pastures on a tractor. Then I'd spend the second half of the day, every day, staining the 12-mile-long post-and-beam wood fence that crisscrossed the property. Over those few summers, I spent over a thousand hours just painting that fence.

Ultimately, I was fortunate to have these jobs when I was young. They were tough, and I hated them, but it's not like I was foraging for food or had to earn enough to feed a family. I was a student who was lucky enough to get everything he needed and the money I earned was my own. These jobs provided the foundation of the strong work ethic I have today. Sitting in my New York City apartment, my father transformed the meaning of Work for me. I suddenly understood that, in the past, I was working for the *job*. I was earning money so I would have pocket money in college, or so I could move to New York City after graduation. Now I was working for the *career*—it was no longer only about a paycheck. It was about something much bigger. Our careers are a huge part of our lives. Since most of us must work for a living, shouldn't that work enrich our lives and inspire us to do bigger and better things while making money at the same time?

My dad thought it was pointless for me to complain that I didn't have a business degree. I was in sales. That ultimately meant I was in the "people brokering" business, and that was something I could master no matter what school I went to or where I was from. I didn't have to create my product, I just had to sell it. I understood that I wasn't a broker of real estate, I was a broker of people's wants and desires. I had been thinking about my Work all wrong. I was complaining about the grind—the hours, frustrations, and uncertainty—because I was focused on the job. I wasn't thinking big enough. Sure, I was selling more at that time because I wanted to be successful and earn more money, but until I had clarity on what I was working for, I was going to feel stressed and overwhelmed. It really got me thinking. Why do I want to do this? What pushes me? What is my ultimate goal in life? These are big questions, and taking the time to dig deep and dissect the answers can be your best gifts to yourself and your career. I know what my Work really entails—everything that the Finder, Keeper, and Doer in me does every day. I know Why I do it. I know what Wall my back was up against to get here. And, ultimately, I know what my Win is! I know exactly what I want all this to add up to at the end of my life. These four tenets opened up a new and unexpected path to success for me. And to think that when my parents came to visit that fall I thought we'd just catch up and hang out together after I'd spent several days all by myself, in total darkness, without a working cell phone to keep me connected to humanity.

THE FOUR W'S

I'm going to do you a favor right now and tell you the most important thing you can do to improve your sales. Do whatever you want with this book. But if you do anything, please define your four tenets.* Not only will you sell more and enjoy greater success, but if you do this you will lead a more fulfilling life. Do you ever wake up nervous and feeling lost? Do you come home feeling exhausted, but you can't pinpoint exactly why you are so tired? By defining your Four Tenets, you will wake up easier and walk lighter. You will have a clear purpose during your day, your week, your month, and throughout your entire year. You will never doubt why you do what you do, and why you are working so hard for it every single day. I wish I had figured this out sooner! I've thought back to when I was working out what my tenets were, and I'm going to guide you through the same process below. Please know, though, that I'm here to help—we can work on these together. Seriously, email me at ryan@ryanserhant.com.

Tenet #1: The Why

WHY DO YOU DO WHAT YOU DO?

Knowing why I get up every morning to work so hard, go to so many appointments, and most days eat lunch in my car to sell real estate is crucial to my success. Why do I do it? Why sales? There are so many career paths I could have followed. I could have been a lawyer (though I actually bombed my LSAT, so maybe not) or a banker—but I *chose sales*. I believe I chose a job in sales because there is no ceiling, and what's better to a born competitor than a career field that presents an endless amount

---

* I am evangelical when it comes to the Four Tenets. If you want to change your career and sell more today, do this right *now*.

of opportunity? I am the engineer of my own destiny. I have the freedom to sell whatever I want and as much as I want. I would have reached the end of that fence in Colorado eventually, but there will never be that moment in my sales career.

Is your Why big enough and powerful enough to sustain you on those days when life is pushing back at you? There are days when things that should be so simple become incredibly complex and frustrating for me. Like the client who doesn't understand that their apartment isn't selling because they overpriced it, or when I don't get a listing I want and I know I'm the best broker for it. These are the days when it would be tempting to tell Emilia to pack a bag and we'd just drive over the George Washington Bridge right out of New York City and never look back. See ya, suckers! Serhant is *out*. But my Why—and my very supportive wife—always pushes me forward, fuels me, and gets me back on the road. It urges me to power through and keep moving forward no matter what is going on (dead deals, client madness, exhaustion, etc.). I know the difficult moment will pass (never fast enough) and I will sell more, close more deals, and all will be well again. There is no ceiling to what I can achieve! To find your why, ask yourself…

Why do I breathe? No, no, don't laugh. Ask yourself easy questions first. So you can live. Ditto food and water. Being alive is good! Stretch your answer beyond the obvious—it's a fact that humans need money to live. Why do you work in sales? What will keep you going when work is throwing rotten tomatoes at you? What thoughts propel you to keep moving forward in your career, no matter what?

Ryan's WHY: *I am a born competitor and sales has zero ceiling; there is always more to reach for. This thought pushes me forward on challenging days.*

Your WHY: *Write down what keeps you going, no matter what.*

_____

_____

_____

_____

Tenet #2: The Work

WHAT DO YOU DO EVERY DAY TO EXPAND YOUR BUSINESS?

I had already learned early on that selling apartments wasn't about opening doors, flipping a light switch, and pointing to a bedroom. I mean, yes, technically there is some Doer work that needs to happen to sell an apartment, but that is not the real Work that goes into making my career successful. My dad was absolutely right when he said I was in the people-brokering business. My Work is about connecting clients to a product they want, their dream home—a place where they can live comfortably and create memories. To do that, I have to listen and empathize. To continue making sales I have to maintain and cultivate personal relationships. Your Work, at its core, needs to elevate your career to the next level—these are the things that are bigger than the physical work or daily tasks you do during the day. To discover your real work, ask yourself…

What am I really selling? You aren't just selling wedding gowns; you are selling dreams and a new chapter in someone's life! How do you do that? If you're a bookseller, you're not just selling books. You're selling an escape—an opportunity to be swept away to another world. How do you connect a reader with the perfect book when there are so many options to choose from? What does that Work look like? Where do you begin? Don't let fear hold you back. Break down what you'd need to do to be the best salesperson ever. What can you start doing, right now—*this very second*—to push your career to new heights?

Ryan's WORK: *Every day is about working to expand my thriving sales business. I must constantly seek out new projects, discover new strategies for marketing myself so I can cast my net wider.*

Your WORK: *What can you start doing right now to grow bigger and better?*

_____

_____

_____

_____

Tenet #3: Your Wall

WHAT ARE YOU RUNNING FROM?

My former coworker Ben Kennedy (thanks, Ben, wherever you are!) taught me about my Wall. This has been invaluable to me. While I'll never know for sure what was pushing Ben, it could have been having to return to a small life in a small town like me, or something worse. My back was up against a Wall when I was hiding my tears on the subway because my credit card was declined at the grocery store for a cup of yogurt. I never wanted to be in that situation again, and this fear propelled me to work harder and get the hell away from that Wall. My first Wall was easy to identify—not having enough money to buy groceries. It felt terrible! I'm proud to be able to say that after many years working in sales, my Wall no longer involves financial stress.

I'm still careful with how I spend my money (and I always will be), but now I know that whatever I do buy, I'll be able to work hard and make sure it's paid for. Now my Wall has shifted to something that's become even more important to me. My Wall is now about using all my potential. I. Can't. Stand. The idea of not milking my potential for all it's worth. Just thinking about it actually makes me feel sick! I want to wake up every day and do a little bit more than I did the day before. And, to be clear, this isn't limited to making money. Maybe I'll write something today that really helps another salesperson or, who knows, maybe an episode of my vlog will inspire someone to go work in sales... that would be *awesome*. Should I get run over by a taxi tomorrow (which would suck), I want to know I did everything in my power to be the absolute best version of myself. My biggest fear, and my Wall today, is wasted potential—leaving leftovers on the table. What's your Wall? Ask yourself...

What time in your life do you never want to return to ever again? Whether it was one brief (but totally humiliating) moment, like mine at the grocery store, or maybe you experienced an extended difficulty—like you were totally broke and had to sleep on a friend's couch, or you worried every day about putting food on the table for your family—bring it to the forefront of your mind right now. This is intense stuff! It's never particularly fun to remember our darker moments, but trust me when I tell you that allowing yourself to go back to that time and feel all those feelings can be an incredibly powerful tool for a salesperson. Tell me, what does that moment look like? Describe the scene—what do you see? What are you feeling? Were you scared, hurt, embarrassed, terrified, or totally humiliated? Maybe a hideous cocktail of all the aforementioned feelings? I know it sucks to remember, but, if you can, take all those feelings and channel them into a fierce desire to move yourself to a better and brighter place. Every time a little voice in your head says, "Wow, this is hard—I'm not doing so great this week," stop right there. Don't dwell on difficult times, but the simple act of reminding yourself that at *this* moment, your back is not against *that* Wall, is an amazing feeling. You've distanced yourself from it, and that will give you the energy to keep going.

Ryan's WALL: *Years ago, it was having my credit card declined at a New York City grocery store. Now wasted potential is what scares me.*

Your WALL: *What is that moment, or day, or mental state you need to distance yourself from forever? I'm asking for very heavy answers. Maybe your last job had you crying at the end of each day—is that what you're running from? Were you in a bad relationship and now you're on your own and don't want to look back? Go ahead and describe it in all its grizzly detail. Then write about how you can distance yourself as far as possible from that moment.*

_____

_____

_____

_____

Tenet #4: The Win

WHAT ARE YOU DOING THIS FOR?

I would like to leave a *very* big impact on the world. It's not just about selling and earning a large income (although those things are enjoyable)—it's about what you're known for when you die. Back to that taxi, the one I hope does not run me over tomorrow—if it did, and the life of Ryan Serhant came to an abrupt end on the corner of Broadway and Houston Street, I'd probably be remembered as that guy who was on that reality TV show about selling high-end real estate in New York. That would be *okay*—I've been incredibly fortunate to be on TV! But I'd like my legacy to be bigger. I'd love to be remembered as the person who changed the way sales is viewed as a profession. It would be awesome if I inspired salespeople to take pride in their work, and I was able to encourage people to fully embrace a job that can be *so* rewarding if you just work for it. How cool would it be if sales was viewed as a super-exciting profession that people couldn't wait to break into? Who cares about glossy fashion magazine writing jobs?! Sales is the place for me! If I could play even a small part in making that happen—that would be a major win.

Before I encourage you to think about your Win, I want to make it clear that a Win is not a reward. A car is a reward. Buying a new suit or a piece of jewelry is a reward—those are not wins. Rewards are something you buy for yourself because you are either gifting or incentivizing yourself. It's perfectly acceptable to give yourself a reward. A Win is something bigger. A Win is the legacy you leave behind. And your Win doesn't have to be as big as "change the world"—but it needs to be real, it needs to change *you*, and it needs to be something you really *want*. Are you a struggling mother of two and you aspire to provide well for your kids and maybe even pay for their college education in full to set them on the right path? So when they come home in their early 30s, they can afford to take care of *you*—that's a Win. Ask yourself…

What's the conversation you'd like people to have about you when you're not around? Be honest: What would you like people to say? That you were an awesome sales machine? That you had a great tax return one year? That you inspired your team and you achieved great things together? That you came up with the most creative pitches and always had a fresh approach to selling? That you connected so effortlessly with customers? Think big! What is the legacy you'd like to leave behind? What kind of mark do you want to make on the world? And don't say you can't think that big. You're human, you have a brain, and you're reading a book about how to be a better salesperson so you can make more money and lead a more fulfilling life. THINK BIG. Ask yourself... What's your Win?

Ryan's WIN: *Changing the way people view sales so that everyone in the world will want to work in a job that offers limitless possibilities.*

Your WIN: *What do you want people to say about you when you're not in the room? What's the big mark you want to leave on the world? Don't hold back!*

_____

_____

_____

_____

After my dad blew my mind, my attitude shifted. It wasn't just a way to work harder; this was about building a career I could be proud of. My mind-set shifted from "This is what I need to do to sell—get up early and work a ton of hours" to "This is what I'm going to do to build an amazing career." My career wasn't all about earning money, although that certainly was part of the equation. I was pushing myself to think about what I could do to be the best salesperson I could be. The four tenets are the building blocks that get me to the next level.

POSITIVITY:
THE OIL THAT KEEPS EVERYTHING RUNNING

I've known what my four tenets are for a long time, but there have still been moments in my career when I've felt beyond challenged, and staying positive, along with the support of my wife, are the only things that keep it all from falling apart. Positivity can seriously save your ass.

Five years ago, I pitched my heart out to the Colonnade Group who had a building I wanted to sell. I kept refreshing my email like a freak, hoping to get an email saying I'd gotten the job. When I found out they were going with someone else, I was devastated. Fast-forward four years, and they call me. The penthouse still hasn't sold, we're asking $7 million, would you like to try to sell it? YES, I would! I throw myself into the Work. I stage the apartment—it looks *amazing*—and market the hell out of it. I'm thrilled this listing has come back to me full circle, and It. Will. Sell. Month one goes by with no offers. Sigh. Months two, three, and four? Zero offers. Now I'm getting nervous. My exclusive agreement is about to expire, and I get the dreaded phone call that they'll be using someone else. Most brokers would have thought, "That's fine, it's not selling—I'll let it go." Most brokers would have had an excuse—it's the market, it's too hot outside, Mercury is in retrograde! But not me. Deep in my core I believed I could sell this apartment. I was positive I could. Ready, set, GO! I called everyone. I spent the entire day emailing and calling people, trying to find a buyer. I never stopped believing I could pull this off. And it worked—I found one! After two weeks of negotiations, contracts were signed. Sold! To celebrate, I popped by the apartment and jumped on top of the counter (I made sure my shoes were clean first) to take a picture for Instagram so I could shout about this sale to the world. Follow-up, perseverance, and hard work matter—but sometimes a deal is so challenging that your positivity is the only thing that can get you through. When it looked like I was going to lose the listing (again), I didn't waste an ounce of energy on fear or doubt. I shifted everything into high gear, staying positive until we had a signed contract.

Be positive, ignore all the reasons it seems like something can't be done—focus on what you can do, right now, to get the deal done. When it feels like nothing is working, your positivity can give you just the boost you need to work a little harder, make one more phone call, reach out to one more person, or try just one more thing—and, suddenly, when it feels like all is lost, you've closed your deal.

I really don't know anything about jazz. But I do know that a famous trumpeter named Roy Hargrove, who skyrocketed to the top of his game at a young age, said something very wise that I'll always remember. He said, "If you're gonna be a musician, you've got to be open. Don't leave anything out. If you take care of the music, it will take care of you." I love this quote because what Hargrove expressed so beautifully about his music is exactly how I feel about my work as a salesperson. If I take care of the work, the work will take care of me. Think about it. Life is going to go up and down. You will have great days and some you'd like to forget ever happened. You will have good relationships and bad ones. It's all inevitable. But if you stay positive, stay thankful, and you take care of the Work, the work will take care of you. But first you must truly understand what your work entails. For Hargrove, his Work is changing the face of music one song at a time, and it gets him through the shit. Please, before you move onto the next chapter, pound out your four tenets—and let your work take care of you.

THE SERHANT WAY

If you do anything at all from this book, please take the time to think about your four tenets and write down your thoughts in the space provided in the chapter. I draw strength from mine regularly, and I'm not kidding when I say that doing this can change your life. It was revolutionary for me to truly understand the difference between working for the job and working for the career! Knowing my Why and my Win reminds me why all this hard work and effort matter! And remembering my Wall makes me feel gratitude about where I am in life today, but also makes it much easier to get out of bed and get to work in the morning. I couldn't afford yogurt! I also make a point of revisiting my tenets because reminding myself why I do all this keeps me centered, focused, and inspired to work harder and achieve more. And don't forget that your answers might change over time, and that's fine! Make revisiting and refining your tenets a regular part of your sales practice.

Tenet #1: The Why: *Why do you do what you do?*
Tenet #2: The Work: *What do you do every day to expand your business?*
Tenet #3: Your Wall: *What are you running from?*
Tenet #4: The Win: *What are you doing this all for?*

Positivity: Don't underestimate the power of positivity. It's the oil that keeps it all running smoothly.

CHAPTER 8

Be the One Who...

A tale of two brownstones.

I once listed two brownstones for sale on the same block, at the same time, for about $10 million each. These balls were very similar, but had some interesting differences.

The first listing, on West 87th Street, was the best of brownstones. It was as if 1884 and 2017 had had a baby—and that baby was awesome. It had been meticulously restored by an amazing developer. It had original fireplaces, rococo ceilings, and mahogany wood as far as the eye could see. It also had a beautiful modern kitchen, eight perfect bathrooms, a massive roof deck with outdoor heating, and an elevator so you could ride up and down, stopping to admire each floor of your ridiculously cool house.

I wouldn't say the second listing was the worst of brownstones—it had all the charming old details that people expect from a brownstone on the Upper West Side, like pocket doors and high ceilings, original crown moldings, and a parlor for drinking tea and smoking cigars while wearing slippers. But unlike its better-appointed neighbor just down the block, it wasn't staged—there was no furniture at all. It didn't have an elevator or a roof deck. Selling an empty house that looked sad and abandoned would normally be almost impossible. Except it wasn't, because it was Billie Holiday's house. No roof deck? Who cares? You can tell people that "Lady Day" had swingin' cocktail parties in your house with lots of famous jazz musicians. I mean, whoever had originally lived at the better brownstone was probably just a normal, non-famous, musically challenged pedestrian like the rest of us. Whoever bought Billie Holiday's house wasn't just buying a home, she was also buying a unique piece of history—and that history never changes. The next buyer, and the buyer after that, all get to say things like, "Do you agree that Billie Holiday's rendition of George Gershwin's 'Summertime' is unparalleled? Am I right? Oh, did I mention this was Billie Holiday's house?" That is a cool story. And it's the kind of story that sells a house. Even one that's empty.

I never forget that I'm not really selling a product; I'm selling a product's story. Obviously, not every house I sell was once inhabited by a legendary jazz singer. But a home is a great big ball of emotion—it's not an ordinary purchase. It's the place where you'll relax and catch up on *Game of Thrones* after a long day and where your future children will trip over furniture while learning to walk. But nearly every purchase we make is tied to a feeling. The shoes we choose to buy send signals about who we are, like, "Whoa. He's fancy." Or, "Those are sensible clogs. You must be a nurse or a lunch lady or Mario Batali." People want to feel good about what they've purchased. You want to be able to tell your friends you got a great deal on your car, or you just bought the same kind of golf clubs that Rory McIlroy uses—or maybe that your wedding dress was made by the same designer who made Kate Middleton's third cousin's wedding gown! You can create that essential connection between the product and the

customer by relaying a story. At the end of the day, that's ultimately all anyone wants—a good bedtime story. Crafting that
story isn't always as simple as saying, "You know who loves these
socks? George Clooney!" More often you have to get creative and
dig deep, learning as much as you can about your product to find
that little seed of a story, because a good story is exciting. And
when you sell excitement, you can sell anything—even an empty,
sad old house.

Serhant Secret #16

Go beyond the facts. When selling any product,
sell it with a story. You'll close more deals and quickly.

EVERY PRODUCT HAS A STORY—
YOU JUST HAVE TO FIND IT

Meet John Deco

When I was 25, I became one of New York City's youngest sales
directors of a building, 99 John Street. I was incredibly excited
and insanely nervous. It was 442 apartments, nearly a half-
billion-dollar sellout, and a lot of pressure. And I had never done
anything like that before. This was a huge opportunity, but only
if I could figure out how to actually sell the apartments. This
was a short time after the financial markets collapsed in 2008,
and the homes weren't selling—which is how I got the project
in the first place. The developer had an on-site sales team that

had sold almost nothing, and they needed someone hungry who was going to "create the market." Brokers had written the building off—no one was even coming to see it. I needed to find a way to put a fresh spin on this building so I could get some traffic going.

I decided to start by learning as much about the building as I could. When I googled it, lots of information came up about the 442 units being developed into condos. Nothing interesting about that! When the market is great, that's all you need. But when the market is bad, you need to sell more than just the product—you need to sell the story. I wanted to find that special nugget of information that would make people get excited about coming to see it—like George Washington once stayed here, or Justin Bieber. Then I found it. I discovered that 99 John Street was designed by Shreve, Lamb and Harmon. What? Who are they? Oh, just the architects who designed a little art deco marvel known as the Empire State Building. These architects were big names in the art deco movement of New York City. The art deco movement is associated with beautiful architecture, glamour, cocktails, and people enjoying cigarettes because they didn't yet know that smoking was going to kill them. The art deco roots of 99 John Street were unique, and gave me something to work with. I called my friend from college, Tom Booth,* who is a talented illustrator. He created a silhouette of a man with a cool Humphrey Bogart–style hat, and we named him John Deco.

John Deco became the basis of our marketing campaign. We decided to throw John Deco a homecoming party as our launch

---

* Look him up. He's awesome. http://www.tom-booth.com

event. We invited a lot of brokers for food and drinks, and gave out fancy gifts from Tiffany & Co. and Hermès, making sure everyone knew that both of those stores were located right in the area. See what a great neighborhood this is!? Now people were talking about the building. Suddenly, instead of calling the building 99 John, brokers started referring to it as "the John Deco building." It was no longer just a bunch of units being converted into condos—now everyone knew about the building's rich history because we had created a story to showcase it to potential buyers. We got our first three offers the next day.

USING A **STORY** TO CRAFT A CREATIVE PITCH

Step One: Clearly Define Your Challenge

My problem was that no one was paying attention to this building anymore. It was a tough market, and it didn't stand out. It was essentially just another building being converted into condos. I needed to find a fresh way to get people talking about it.

Step Two: Dig In

Go beyond the basic facts about your product. What is the history of your product and can you use it to tell an interesting story for a fresh pitch? 99 John was built by a legendary architectural firm who had built some of New York City's most prized architectural gems. This is an interesting piece of history unique to 99 John Street. Do you sell hand lotion? Who invented hand lotion and why? How far has hand lotion technology come? "Did you know Native Americans used to moisturize with boiled-down animal fat? Isn't this a great time to be alive? Our two-for-one product has no animal fat. Have four bottles."

Step Three: Plant the Seed

How can you use this story in a creative way to make people want the product? I was able to use the fact that the building was a great example of art deco architecture to make it stand out from other, more generic developments. We used the history to create the image of John Deco, who became the basis for our fresh new marketing campaign. We had an interesting story to share with buyers. Sell insurance? Having a hard time convincing people they *need* insurance? Here's a seed: "Did you know that insurance dates back to the dawn of humanity, when neighbors would insure each other with a place to live should something happen to their homes? Survival of the fittest, with the insurance of the buddy system. Now I know you probably don't want your wife moving in with Ted next door should your house collapse on top of you, making her a widow. Isn't this a great time to be alive? The premium on our life insurance is 25 percent off today only."

PRODUCT **KNOWLEDGE** EQUALS POWER

I met Frank when he asked for my help selling kitchen cabinets, and we decided to film his story for *Sell It Like Serhant*. Frank was a real character—he was like something out of *A Bronx Tale*. He was super easy to talk to, but for some reason he couldn't close a deal. He was great at connecting with customers, but when they started to ask questions he'd often step away and ask a colleague to come help. As a starting point, I wanted Frank to tell me a little about his product. When I asked him what the cabinets were made out of, he shrugged and said, "Um, wood?" Ohhhh. Okay. It quickly became clear that Frank didn't know anything about his product, other than that cabinets were things you put in kitchens to store boxes of cereal. Until Frank had better product knowledge he wouldn't be confident answering any questions—and who wants to buy their kitchen from that guy? People want to spend their money with the most confident and most knowledgeable person, otherwise they will just stay home and shop on the internet. And right now, Frank was not beating the internet.

Serhant Secret #17

If you want to learn how to sell a meal, you've got to spend some time in the kitchen. If it's possible to see how your product is produced firsthand, do it!

We took a road trip to Pennsylvania, where Frank's company got the lumber for their cabinets. We watched as giant trees were taken down and cut into planks (and they let me hold a chain saw!). Then the wood was dried in a special process that could take up to two years. The cabinets were carefully handcrafted by actual human beings—these were some seriously next-level cabinets. Now Frank could answer questions about his product with more than a one-word response (wood). And his newfound knowledge about the intricacies of cabinetmaking provided a good starting point for a story. He could talk to customers about the quality of their product, how the cabinets are custom-made from hand-cut, cured wood—and that his company had been making cabinets this way since the 1950s. These weren't cheap cabinets you'd have to put together yourself—puzzling over vague instructions for hours, only to end up with a crooked kitchen that gives your house a condemned look. *These* cabinets were the best. They were designed to house your family's Cocoa Puffs and Yodels for generations to come! Frank's newfound product knowledge enabled him to craft a compelling pitch: These cabinets are hand-built from solid hardwood (unlike most cabinets made of less durable pine), using traditional old-world techniques. These cabinets are one of the best investments you can make in your home, as they are built to last your family a lifetime. We've been installing them in beautiful kitchens around New York City for over 50 years. SOLD!

USING THE **PRODUCT** TO CRAFT A CREATIVE PITCH

Step One: Clearly Define Your Challenge

Frank's challenge was that there are now countless places to buy kitchen cabinets—big box stores, the internet, and, to complicate things further, his cabinets (while worth every penny) were a larger investment than some of the other options out there. How could he clearly show customers the true value of his product?

Step Two: Dig In

On our road trip, Frank learned firsthand why his product requires a larger investment than his competitors'—his product was handmade, in America, in a detailed process that's taken several generations to perfect. He wasn't selling cheap crap— he was selling the Rolls Royce of cabinets. But now that Frank had seen the care and craftsmanship that went into building his product, he could use this knowledge when talking to customers. He now understood these weren't ordinary kitchen cabinets.

Step Three: Plant the Seed

Now Frank could build a story and pitch around the fact that he's seen how his product is built (by skilled human beings!) and knows that it's a superior option and the cabinets will last a lifetime. He can use this information to create a story that will appeal to a homeowner's emotions—that these cabinets had been carefully crafted using the same old-school techniques for over 50 years.

Using creativity to craft a story or pitch is a really fun process, and I've used it countless times. Enjoy being creative—it will help you attract shiny new balls, get publicity, and close deals. Once I hired an artist to paint the naked bodies of models and then made a 100-foot-long banner out of the images and hung it on the building I was selling to create buzz. It worked. People talked about it, and the building sold. We weren't just another boring new condo project. Once I was selling an apartment with zero views. It literally faced a brick wall. This apartment was ideal for someone who didn't care about light (like maybe a vampire). I staged a glow-in-the-dark party to show how perfect this apartment was for people who were only home late at night. And it worked. It sold. I embraced the totally dated 1980s décor in a townhouse by throwing an '80s party and arriving in a DeLorean. It sold in one day for $7.5 million. There are no limits to how you can use creativity to highlight what is interesting or unique about a product so that people will want to buy it.

EVERY SALESPERSON NEEDS A HOOK

Anthony Hopkins is a well-respected actor who has played Richard Nixon and C. S. Lewis—very serious roles. But when you see Sir Anthony Hopkins, Commander of the Order of the British Empire, on the screen, the first thing you probably think is, "Wow, that guy he's standing next to better watch out, because Hopkins is probably going to eat his face." When we see Anthony Hopkins we don't say, "He's the one who played the butler in that stunning Merchant Ivory picture." We say, "That's the serial killer who ate people's livers with a side of fava beans and a nice glass of Chianti." Hopkins is known as the One Who Played Hannibal Lecter.

I started out as the One Who asked pregnant women at Starbucks if they needed more space. And while there is an abundance of pregnant women in New York City, I knew that if I wanted to be successful, I'd have to expand beyond being the one who found new apartments for families looking to upgrade. I was not going to be satisfied with the success that came along with renting two-bedroom apartments—I wanted the kind of success that came from selling multimillion-dollar apartments every day.

In sales, there is a direct correlation between the business that you get and the business you're known for. So how do you make the shift from the person you are now (the person who sells a little) to the person you want to be—the one who sells A LOT, ALL THE TIME. The decision I made to become a broker who sells seven- and eight-figure apartments took time. A lot of time. But I followed a few core ideas to become the One Who sells multimillion-dollar apartments.

Establish Your Base Camp: Create a Hook and Get Ready to Climb

Your first hook as a salesperson is that special thing about you. It's what makes someone want to buy from you, rather than anyone else. When Frank and I got back from our road trip to Pennsylvania, we worked on what made him the *best* person to buy cabinets from. Frank decided his hook was that he was the "soup to nuts" kitchen guy. He was the guy who vowed to work with customers until their dream kitchen was finished. He'd guide them throughout the entire process—from picking out the cabinets, to measurements and installation, right up until the moment those cabinets were filled with coffee cups. He wasn't going to sell you some cabinets and then ditch you to figure the rest out on your own—Frank's thing was that he stuck around.

Who you are as a salesperson today may not be who you are tomorrow, or next year. Sure, for now Frank is the "soup to nuts" kitchen guy, and that's great. But should Frank be hanging out at a neighborhood barbecue when he's introduced to Joe, the Guy

Who Owns 50 Apartment Buildings, then Frank should become the One Who arranges for high-quality kitchen cabinets to be installed in large apartment buildings. His sales would instantly increase. Becoming the best salesperson means having a hook but also being flexible, and open to playing with different kinds of balls. In a million years, I would have never imagined I'd be known as the One Who breaks real estate sales records in Brooklyn. Selling real estate in Brooklyn has become a huge part of my business, and had I not been willing to change from being the One Who sells apartments in Manhattan to the guy who also sells them in Brooklyn, I would have missed out on a massive opportunity for myself and my team. Your original hook is your starting point, but don't be afraid to change it—as the wind blows, you go.

Shout It from the Mountaintop: Success Begets Success

As I was transitioning from the One Who rents two-bedrooms to expectant parents, I shouted to the entire world about any big deal I made. Sure, for a long time the bulk of my deals were rentals, with an occasional sale sprinkled in here and there. But I did not wait until I got to where I am today to shout about being the "billion-dollar broker." That would have made zero sense. If you make a big sale, you're one step closer to being the salesperson you want to be. Let everyone know about it. Send out postcards, post on social media, talk about it every chance you get. No one else but yourself (or maybe your mother) is going to shout about your accomplishments.

Once I decided to be a real estate agent, I knew I wanted to be the one who sells multimillion-dollar apartments. But I didn't wake up one day and say, "Well, I've had it with the $2,000 per month rentals. I know! I'll just stalk people on Park Avenue until someone agrees to let me sell their $20 million penthouse today." While it would have been fun to try, chances are it would have resulted in a restraining order. I was nailing the $2,000 per month apartments. So instead of looking for more of that business, I actively searched for people I could rent $3,000 apartments to—and then $4,000. I wasn't making giant career leaps—that's a futile effort. I was taking baby steps. The conversation with the customer who buys a $3,000 hot tub is very similar to the one who buys a $4,000 one. Same amount of work, knowledge, time, and effort—but you make more money, slowly. Then $4,000 becomes $5,000, and so on until you only get out of bed for the Mac Daddy $15,000 hot tub daydream. In sales, success begets success. Now that I was renting to people who had larger budgets, they were referring their friends to me who had equally large—or even larger—budgets. Then one day one of those customers saw that it would be cheaper per month to own than to rent. And, just like that, I now only worked in sales. Even to this day I'm always thinking about what ball I can reach for next. What business am I not doing right now that I should be doing? Cast yourself as the One Who does bigger and better things that you could never have imagined, and do them.

Embrace Longevity: Enjoy the View from the Top

While I embrace growth—expansion in all ways, please!—I also acknowledge that, for a salesperson, ultimately being known for one big thing is great. It means you've made it to the top. Being typecast as an actor isn't ideal. Can you even imagine what would happen if Will Ferrell played Hannibal in *Hannibal Lecter Part Four: The Final Meal*? He could do a scene where he eats someone's appendix and we'd all think it was hilarious. Will Ferrell is one of the funniest human beings alive and it would be hard for us to view him as a deranged cannibal. But if you've reached a level where you're typecast for what you sell and you're happy with it, it's a great thing. You sell diamonds, but only above three carats? Awesome, you're the Woman Who sells huge diamonds. You sell outdoor movie theatres, but they start at six figures and you work with a landscaper to have them installed on estates in the Hamptons? Great, you're the One Who sells insane outdoor cinemas. Once you're happy about what and who you're selling to, embrace it and enjoy it and be ready to move with the wind.

WHEN YOU'RE AT WORK, YOU ARE AT WORK

I need to be very clear about something. When you are at work you need to act like you're at work. The store is open? *You* are open. Thousands of struggling salespeople reached out to me about coming on my show *Sell It Like Serhant*. Ultimately, eight people made it onto the first season. Each one of these salespeople was in danger of losing his or her job, and all of them had different challenges to conquer. Some people, like Frank, had zero product knowledge, while others struggled to make personal connections with potential customers. But there was one common thread I saw across the board that drove me bananas. Unless they were face-to-face directly with a customer, they weren't *on*. And when a salesperson is at work, you are at work. You're not eating a bagel or scrolling through your ex's Instagram—you are on and ready to make a sale.

On the first day of filming each episode, I would walk into the store to observe the salesperson I'd be working with. I made sure they didn't know I was watching (I'm sneaky). Every single time I saw the same thing. The salesperson was sitting and waiting, shoulders hunched over, no smile in sight. Worse than that, half the people I worked with were in a corner somewhere on their phone. They weren't interacting with clients, even just saying something simple like, "Hello, beautiful day." Or "Hey, we have this amazing new lavender body scrub in! You've got to smell it!" You can't wait for the perfect opportunity to arise to initiate a connection or start selling. That's not how you build a sales career.

Remember dial-up internet? Cue AOL's "You've got mail" notification. These days the internet is always on and it has changed the world! Information, connection, a new sweater, and your favorite song are always at your fingertips. That's how salespeople need to be!

If your inner salesperson is always on, you can change the world. You are always prepared, ready to go—you don't wait for a customer to appear in front of you before you flip a switch and are open for business. Successful salespeople are always on.

I'm not saying you should stand on the street 12 hours a day with a freaky smile and demand that people buy doughnuts from you. I'm saying just because a customer is *not* in front of your face, that does not give you a ticket to do nothing. If you learn anything from this book, it's that there is so much to do when the customer isn't there to build your sales numbers! In fact, when you're alone is the best time to be a salesperson! We can prospect for new clients for 30 minutes, send follow-up, follow-through, and follow-back emails and texts for another 30 minutes, and strategize with our manager on an incentive-of-the-day to offer to customers if they buy TODAY. Trolling Facebook for an hour is only OK if you're finding clients.

Serhant Secret #18

No customers in front of you? This is an excellent opportunity to get work done.

LET YOUR INNER FREAK FLAG FLY
(AND HAVE FUN)

You never know what you're going to find when a client opens the door. As a broker, I've walked into rooms and found giant piles of creepy doll heads and sculptures made out of garbage. Once I was talking to a Wall Street trader about what he wanted in a new apartment when a kangaroo bounced out of his bedroom and hopped across his loft. Brokers see weird things. But I was still surprised when Patty, this tiny Chinese grandmother, opened the large closet in her spare bedroom. From floor to ceiling it was packed full of ribbons, bows, and lace in every imaginable color. It was like Hello Kitty and Snow White got high together and decided to open an Etsy shop. This little lady—who negotiated like a seasoned Wall Street ballbuster, by the way—had a passion for making hair bows. I closed the door and hoped potential buyers wouldn't be turned off by Patty's psychedelic ribbon cave. I was lucky. I was able to sell Patty's apartment at full asking price in less than a day. But there was a catch. The buyer wanted Patty (and her ribbons) out within 30 days. That meant if I didn't want to lose the sale, I'd have to find Patty an apartment immediately. But Patty hated everything I showed her. One apartment was too cramped, one was too close to the building next door, and she hated one so much that she turned around and left without even walking inside. I was starting to worry I'd lose the buyer we had for Patty's apartment, and my two sales would turn to zero sales. I had to do everything in my power to urge Patty out of the disappointment stage—and fast.

I found a listing in Battery Park City that I thought was perfect. But with the days ticking by I wasn't going to take any chances. I had to make Patty fall in love with this apartment and her hobby gave me an idea. I wanted to sell Patty on the apartment by showing her she could have an entire room devoted to her bow-making passion. I bought ribbons. A lot of ribbons. I arrived at the apartment early and set up a table in one of the bedrooms. I filled it with baskets of ribbon in every size and color. Patty could make bows for every princess-loving child in America, and have enough left over to make awards for ponies and Russian gymnasts.

I felt hopeful when Patty walked into the apartment and didn't say she hated anything. She thought the living room was a good size and felt the building next door was far enough away so that no one could spy on her. When I opened the door to the secret ribbon room, Patty's eyes got as wide as saucers and I knew she was going to buy it. She didn't even flinch when I put a bow on my head and told her the price was final and there would be No Negotiating Whatsoever. Patty had found her bow-topia and

I was making a double commission. It was a blue-ribbon day all around.

WHAT'S THE ICING ON THE CAKE?

Setting up a miniature ribbon factory for Patty was creative, and it worked. There was no way I could have known this at the time, but oddly enough the first flicker that creativity could be used to increase my sales happened at that strip club with Sarah. Seeing Sarah's admiration for and appreciation of the dancers showed me something interesting about who she was as a person and where she was in her life—and paying attention to this was almost like receiving a map that guided me to the perfect apartment for Sarah. While I couldn't find Patty an apartment above a ribbon shop (yes, I looked), I could make use of these careful observations to help her see that this apartment was perfect for her in every way. Patty did not have "ribbon cave" listed on her wish list for her perfect home. But I could see she valued her time crafting—it was meaningful to her. The ribbons were the icing on top of the cake that was the right-sized three-bedroom apartment with perfect light in a great neighborhood. It was the ribbons that made the cake irresistible to Patty. Since making deals for Sarah and Patty, I'm always on the lookout for creative things I can do to get people comfortable with the purchase they are about to make.

If your client is stuck in one of the trickier stages of the sale, and you need to urge them forward, dig deep. Is there something she might want that extends beyond the typical? For example, if I have a client who loves to cook and is afraid to commit to an apartment, I might bring her fresh produce from the local farmers' market to show her an added benefit to taking the home. Always be thinking about extra incentives you can offer, no matter how small they may be. Chances are your jewelry store won't let you discount a diamond, but maybe you can offer free cleanings for life. You can guarantee to your clients that their diamonds will never stop sparkling! If you sell dollhouses, throw in a miniature kitten! Sometimes an added incentive isn't just about the object or service itself, it's about how it makes your client feel about their purchase.

Here's an example: It's a grey, cold, rainy Saturday afternoon in New York City. For most people, a day like today is ideal for watching Netflix and taking naps, but I put on a coat and head to an open house in Chelsea. There is a new apartment on the market that some of my clients might like, but that's not the only reason I'm choosing to venture out into the rain instead of snuggling with Emilia at home. I know that channeling my creativity and staying open to trying new things are critical parts of my success. The great thing about creativity is that it has zero limits. It's impossible to tap the bottom of your creativity, and it's impossible to think of everything. There is always another angle, another way, a fresh approach. There's always something else that provides new inspiration. And that's why I'm about to walk into a two-bedroom in Chelsea soaking wet. I want to see how other people sell. I want to know how other brokers do it. I step into a spacious foyer and instantly smell freshly brewed coffee...and wait, are those warm cookies? It's not uncommon to find snacks at an open house, but the combo of good coffee and chocolate chip cookies with soft music playing in the background on one of the grossest days ever immediately gives off a cozy feeling that screams *you are home*. Suddenly, I can see myself coming home to a place like this—I can imagine where I'd put my umbrella and where I'd sit to check my emails and eat dinner with my wife. And I don't even need an apartment! I already have one! The homey feeling the broker has created is distracting everyone from the fact that while the apartment has giant windows in the living room, there's nothing to see outside of them but grey and some more grey. I leave my contact information on the sign-in sheet and about an hour later I receive the Most Comprehensive Follow-up Email in the history of follow-up emails. The broker didn't just text or email a simple, "Hey, thanks for stopping by." She had carefully thought about any question one of my clients might have had about the building, the apartment, and the neighborhood. There were links for everything—she had just made my job much easier and I appreciated that. I wrote her back and told her I didn't have a client for the apartment, but I had a spot for her on my team.

At home that night, I start to think about how I use creativity in my career. I always use creativity to showcase a product and develop pitches and marketing campaigns. But how can I stretch to use my creativity to grow as a salesperson? What can I do that's new and unusual? How can I use creativity to expand my audience and my network? I am so fortunate to be in front of two TV cameras, but maybe it's time for something else. I take a look at my Facebook page, and as I scroll through I see updates and links, and an occasional video. I get out my notebook and open it to my to-do list for the week. I add to my list, "Start a vlog." Then I add another line: "Write a sales book."

THE SERHANT WAY

Don't be afraid to inject creativity and fun into your pitches. Using creativity and stories to sell your product is an excellent tool that will give you a unique edge over your competition.

Crafting a Creative Pitch: Three Easy Steps

1. Identify the challenge.
2. Dig In: What's the history of your product? Or, how is your product produced?
3. Plant the Seed: Grow the nugget of information into a pitch.

Be the One Who: Every Salesperson Needs a Hook

1. Establish Your Base Camp: Create a Hook and Get Ready to Climb
2. Go with the Wind: Be Flexible
3. Shout It from the Mountaintop
4. Climb Higher: Don't Look for the Business You Already Have
5. Embrace Longevity: Enjoy the View from the Top

Using Your Creative Side to Close a Deal

1. Listen carefully and observe.
2. What's the icing on the cake?

CHAPTER 9

How to Fail Smarter

Corfu, Greece, July 7, 2016

I had my tux on and I thought it looked great. Bright blue was the right choice! I did a quick check to make sure nothing was stuck in my teeth and wiped the sweat from my brow. Greece in July equals hot. Everything was in order, and in a few minutes I would board the pirate ship (yes, I said pirate ship) that would take me to an ancient church on a tiny island where I would marry Emilia in front of all our friends and family (and the world, eventually, as Bravo was filming it). Planning a wedding for 150 people on a Greek island was not without its challenges— so when my phone started ringing incessantly, I braced myself for a wedding-related disaster. It could have been anything: the priest was kidnapped, the church had blown up, the extreme heat had caused the guests to break out into a brawl, or we had offended the god Poseidon and he had hurled our wedding cake into the Ionian Sea. I would have preferred it if any of the above had happened (at least it would have made a really good story), rather than what I was about to face.

Let's rewind the story a bit, to my history with Gemma Markelson.

New York City, June 15, 2016

I had been working with Gemma for four years. I had been using all of the Three F's of follow-up, I can promise you. I'd show her an apartment, she'd fall in love, get close to buying it, change her mind, and decide to just keep renting. She was a very loyal client so I never even thought about giving up on her, but she was very picky and she changed her mind a lot. One month she would only want to see apartments with floor-to-ceiling windows and views of the Hudson River. The next month she wanted the same thing, but swap out the Hudson River view with the Empire State Building. Then came the infatuation with open kitchens, followed by a flirtation with a Flatiron loft. There was also the brief phase of "only ground-floor units because it will be easier for my band to practice." What? I had no idea she was in a band. This back-and-forth with Gemma had been going on and off for a long time.

Then, in 2016, about a month before I was going to Greece to get married to the love of my life, I got a great listing on 12th Street. I knew I had the perfect buyer for it—Gemma.

I called her the second I knew I had the listing. She was excited to hear about the exposed brick, the high ceilings, the big master bedroom with an en-suite bathroom and the open layout. It didn't have a view of either a river or a landmark building, but it was well priced and had a huge home office that she could convert to a screening room (or a recording studio). When she walked through the door I noticed that she blushed and smiled—this had never happened before. It was perfect! Gemma had found her home. I had planned to list the apartment for $5 million, but hadn't even put it on the market yet, so I had to make a deal between Gemma and the seller. Enter Gemma's mother:

"Gemma found an apartment? Great! Let's offer $4 million, cash! Closing anytime. Wonderful!" Actually, not wonderful. At this point in the deal (the part where the apartment isn't on the market yet), every seller says The. Exact. Same. Thing: "They want to offer what?!? The apartment isn't even on the market yet—and really, that offer is so low, it's insulting. You haven't even done any work at all. Let's put it on the market and sit back while countless above-asking offers roll in! Find me a Russian billionaire!" To which the buyer always responds: "Why would I increase my offer? It's not even on the market yet. Why would I negotiate against myself? SCREW THAT GUY. Tell him to take it or leave it! Good luck finding a Russian billionaire to overpay!" And I'm in the middle, like a little kid stuck between Mom and Dad, trying to decide the best way to get them to see eye to eye.

Serhant Secret #19

Salespeople often find themselves in the middle of situations that feel impossible—but there's always a solution. Every deal is a deal if you can figure out how to bridge the gap.

My seller and buyer were a million dollars apart—which may seem like a lot, but to me it was just a gap I needed to close. I've learned that this is a crucial moment in every sale. It's in the messy middle, full-on stage three—*fear*. This is where most deals are usually made or lost. The truth was, based on the condition of the apartment and the most recent comparable sales, $5 million was too high, and $4 million was too low, but who cares about facts when you're an oversensitive buyer or seller anyway, right? This meant I had to find a mutually agreeable number for both clients. I had to "bridge the gap," or risk all of us tumbling into the pit of dead deals.

I went to work convincing each party they should make an effort to see if we could reach an agreement. My number one rule at the beginning of any negotiation is to always counter. Clients so often feel there is no point in doing so—they'll say, "We're too far apart, there's no point!" But I've seen time and time again how coaxing two parties to make counters can result in a mutually beneficial transaction where both sides feel they got a good deal (and the broker is happy because he got the sale done). But bridging the gap isn't as simple as coming down or coming up in price. You have to play to the fears. Remember how we discussed having Walls? And the Wall being our motivation to succeed? Buyers and sellers have the same thing. The seller's biggest wall is a future in which they have Not Sold. The buyer's biggest wall is a future in which they have Not Bought. Seems simple, right? I play to those fears in every negotiation. With my seller on 12th Street, I reminded him that the risk of *not* countering was going on the market and not selling at all. Was not selling at all worth not even engaging with this excited, early buyer?

The seller listened to my argument and agreed to reduce the price by $250,000 for "a quick sale." *Yes!* I reminded my buyer this was an off-market deal. She was getting in early, and P.S. her daughter had been searching for an apartment for four years! Wouldn't she like to see her happily settled? She agreed to come up $250,000 for "a quick sale." Just like that, the million-mile distance was slashed in half. I know I'm talking about big numbers here, but what you should understand is that I'm making the gap relative. Whether you're trying to close a million-dollar gap or a $10 one, break it down. I basically asked each side to come up, relatively speaking, $2.50. That doesn't sound nearly as bad as bridging a million-dollar gap, now does it?

We were getting somewhere! Except we weren't there yet—no one wanted to budge an inch further, and no one was ready to agree to the deal either. The seller was thinking, *I just came down a quarter of a million dollars on a place that's not even on the market yet.* While the buyer was thinking—you guessed it, *I just went up a quarter of a million dollars on a place that's not even on the market yet.* I know this seems like an outrageous amount of money, but when the price tag is this high, another $100,000 or so is like caulk in a leaky tub. It's there to patch things together. We had come so far, and I knew we could get to the finish line. That's when I asked the buyer and seller to split the difference. "Meet halfway" is probably the nicest-sounding way of getting a deal done in the history of the negotiation world. Both sides feel good and both sides feel like the other side gave an equal share. They both agreed to come up and down so that the selling price was $4.5 million. Deal! The sellers could move to the house they bought in Connecticut and Gemma would have her screening/band/hamster room.* And best of all, Emilia and I could head to Greece to get married without worrying about any of this. Ha!

---

* She adopted five hamsters over the course of our four-year sales odyssey.

NEGOTIATING TACTICS
THAT CAN KEEP YOUR BALL IN PLAY

If it seems like you are miles away from an agreement, don't be afraid. There are many ways to bridge the gap and find a mutually agreeable situation.

- Always make a counteroffer. You can't get anywhere without a counter.
- Remind clients there is always a cost for time. Time is expensive.
- You can't predict the market. You can't assume there is always a better offer.
- Can the parties involved split the difference?
- Can you as the salesperson offer an additional incentive? Can you lower your commission? Pay for a cost associated with the deal yourself? Remember, $10 is better than $0!

Play the Fears.

- Talk about the Wall—Not Buying and Not Selling.
- Remind the buyer of the risks. Not buying could mean a missed opportunity to buy something they love, get a good price, or purchase something they've been seeking for a long time.
- If you deal with sellers, remind them that going to the market is always risky.

- Emphasize to both parties that the deal can be made right now.

Keep the Conversation Moving.

- To push a ball back into the wind, keep the dialogue moving—even if your client is reluctant to keep talking.
- Listen carefully and craft an appropriate response to your client's concerns.
- Spread the win around: What else can be thrown into the deal to make everyone feel like they are in a winning situation? Example: I once got two parties who were at odds to agree to a deal when the seller threw in the dining-room set for free.

The sellers were excited for their new adventure in Connecticut, and Gemma was working on her co-op board package. The apartment on 12th Street happened to be in a co-op, which meant that she had to be approved by a group of owners, called the board, before the deal could be official and she could close. The co-op board package is a super-invasive rite of passage for most people who buy an apartment in New York City. Buyers must share their entire financial history—salary, tax returns, etc.—with the other owners in the building. If you defaulted on a payment on your Victoria's Secret credit card when you were 23, they'll know about it, and if you're lucky enough to get approved you'll share that shame with them every time you ride the elevator. There's evidence you're mean or insane? You have a yappy dog or you play the tuba as your hobby? They don't like your face? It's Thursday? All reasons you can be denied by an NYC co-op board. But welcome to New York! The co-op board is all-powerful; they can deny you for any reason they want. I got on a plane for Greece knowing Gemma was carefully putting her board package together. All was right in the world. After four years of work with Gemma, I was getting married as a happy salesman.

July 1, 2016. Arrive in Corfu, Greece

And now back to my Big Fat Greek wedding. We had rented the biggest villa in Corfu for two weeks, and we were planning to go crazy having fun and celebrating our love. It's Greece! We had a big welcoming party and all of our family and friends were there. Life was great! But then my seller of the 12th Street loft left a message saying there was a problem. Normally, one of my amazing team members would have taken care of the board package as well as any issues that came up, but this client insisted that I handle everything personally. I had promised Emilia I wouldn't work during our wedding (even though I was kind of already working since I had brought along a film crew), but I hadn't gotten this far in my career by not returning phone calls. Deals die every day— and I fix them! I called my seller. The problem? Since Gemma's parents were gifting the funds for the purchase, and since she was young, and technically unemployed, the co-op wanted all her parents' financial information, too—and her parents didn't want to provide it. To the co-op board, the refusal to provide this information was like a red flag about the size of a Midtown skyscraper. I spent the next couple of days covertly making calls (Emilia would kill me) and going back and forth with the buyer and seller, trying to shepherd them through this process. In the meantime, wedding drama abounds! The church is double-booked! The flowers are trapped in Holland! I'm trying to make sure we have the best wedding ever—but in the back of my mind is this relentless chatter about financial information and co-op board interviews. I try to make myself feel better by reminding myself that I'm attentive and empathetic, and this is just a bumpy ride to a closing…with a $270,000 commission on the line. Breathe.

Serhant Secret #20

One of the reasons you can't live or die by one sale is because you have a life. I will do absolutely everything in my power to close a deal, but I learned at my wedding that I did not want to be ironing out deals while my children were being born, or on my deathbed.

July 7, 2016, 4:48 p.m. Twelve minutes until my wedding.
It turns out I was not receiving a call about a wedding-related disaster. It was just a real estate disaster. *Dammit.* "Hi, Ryan? It's Gemma. So, the board admitted me, but we just aren't comfortable with a building that wants sooo much financial information. So, we don't want to buy it anymore. We're asking for our money back, thanks! And sorry." In that split second, my big commission vanished. I also feared my seller would kill me. Instead of going on the market a month before my wedding, I had encouraged my seller to take this "seamless" off-market transaction. Going back to market in the dead of summer would be a disaster. This means I needed to do damage control quickly.

The seller needs to know about this ASAP since they are ready to move, and this ugly development will ruin their plans. I call my seller to relay the news that their buyer is pulling out. "I'm about to get married in a few minutes, but I'll be back in the city next week and you have my word that I'll find you a new buyer." That wasn't good enough. There was yelling. A lot of it. I tried to explain that the co-op board scared the buyers, and that even though I did everything I could to keep the deal alive, I couldn't control the buyer's feelings. But that wasn't enough. In a dying deal, the salesperson always takes the blame. They didn't want to work with me anymore. Click. Ugh.

While it's frustrating that the deal died, and that it died *during* my wedding, I learned an incredibly important lesson. I felt awful during one of the best weeks in my life. I was supposed to feel incredible! I let my clients control my emotions because I felt indebted to them. When someone hires me to sell their home or represent them in a purchase, it's like life or death for me. I care about the trust these people have invested in me. I felt like I failed them. I worried that no one would want to sell with me again. I started to doubt my own abilities. I think every salesperson has taken a walk down this very dark path at some point. And from that moment on, I decided that dying deals were not going to kill me. I also reminded myself that the loft on 12th Street was not my only ball. When I got back from my wedding there were still many other balls in play. I vowed at that moment to learn something from every single ball that fell flat. Instead of failing hard, I needed to fail smart. This would help me grow as a salesperson and help me prevent other balls from falling in the future.

If you're thinking, "Oh my God, what is wrong with you? You were about to get married to a beautiful woman on a Greek island!" please know that when I got on my pirate ship I left all my problems behind. It was an awesome wedding, and a day I will never forget for all the *right* reasons.

SIX REASONS BALLS FALL AND KILL YOUR DEAL

Everyone drops a ball or has a deal die and it sucks. And if you haven't, you're the first person in the known universe. The deal with Gemma was one of hundreds that I've lost during a ten-year career. And it wasn't even the biggest. I once lost a deal with a $1.2 million commission. Yeah. Ouch. What I've learned is that balls fall for a lot of different reasons, but if you understand the most common deal-killers, you're more likely to be able to keep your balls in the air.

Don't get me wrong—losing a sale is no fun, especially when you've done everything in your power to keep it going. Sometimes I feel like an ER doctor giving CPR to a dead guy—I just want to be able to tell the family I did absolutely everything I could to save him. There really is a bright side to deals dying, though—from failure comes success. I know that sounds like bullshit, but I swear it's true. Even when you've lost money, you've gained experience. Remember 99 John? My first big building, where I learned so much? I was fired from that project. At the time, I thought it was the worst day of my life. But had I *not* been fired, I wouldn't be where I am today. I know that doesn't help when you're trying to pay your mortgage or pay back your student loan, but there will come a time in a sale when you think, "Wait a minute—this is familiar! Oh, wow. I know exactly what to do!" Any sale that doesn't work out is preparing you to close future sales that haven't even happened yet. Let me share with you what I've learned are the six reasons balls crash and die, so you can gain knowledge without experiencing my pain and suffering and keep all your balls in the air. You're welcome!

#1: Failure to Communicate

Lack of communication is the leading cause of death in sales (and any relationship, really). I keep sellers aware of what I'm doing to sell their apartment—holding open houses, advertising and marketing efforts, incoming offers, etc. When I'm trying to sell something to someone, I'm in touch every week about apartments that have just gone on the market, and ones that might be right for them. Keep your customers up-to-date on sales, promotions, and product changes. Touch base regularly so clients know you're taking care of them. If you get fired from a deal, chances are it's because of a breakdown in your communication. If you don't talk to your spouse for a week, it doesn't matter how much you love them in silence—you're going to have problems at home! And by the way, communication is *free*.

#2: You're Replying, Not Responding

Keep the communication flowing so you can get a sense of what stage of the sale your client is facing (excitement, frustration, fear, disappointment, acceptance, happiness, or relief). Listen to your client and address any issues carefully, clearly, and quickly, but do so with care. Most salespeople reply to their clients with standard lines they use on everyone, but the best salespeople listen to their clients and respond thoughtfully. Remember, nearly anything can be bought online today! But the advantage you have as a salesperson is empathy. The internet is not empathetic. The internet can't take a client out for a drink and say, "Listen, I know this process is stressful, but let's talk about it. I just want you to know I hear you and I've got your back." Don't forget to put yourself in your client's shoes from time to time.

#3: You've Set Unrealistic Expectations

I once got fired from a deal in the Hamptons because I was completely wrong about my availability to be physically present on a property. That was my fault for setting unrealistic expectations, and I've never made that mistake again. I'm also careful about setting realistic expectations about pricing. It's so easy to say yes to people, but it causes major problems later. I've gotten comfortable with the idea of having uncomfortable conversations. I won't agree with a client that his apartment should be priced at $12 million when I think it's more like $8 million, just to get a job. If I did that I wouldn't sell the apartment, and the client would be angry—and I promise you he would not remember that the $12 million price tag was his idea. That scenario would end with me getting fired so he could hire a more realistic (and more honest) broker. Make it your policy to be upfront and honest about everything. That includes potential challenges you and your customer could encounter along the way.

#4: You Don't Know Your Shit

When I was new to selling real estate, I had no confidence and zero experience. That's true. But I knew my shit. I couldn't lean on confidence and experience to get me through a showing or a sale—so

I memorized absolutely everything I needed to know about my product. I could rattle off square footages, the year an apartment building was built, what the countertop was made of, the brand of the kitchen appliances, if dogs were allowed, how far the apartment was from the subway, the doorman's name, and how many minutes it would take to walk to get a cup of coffee. Once again, remember why a client is buying from you (and, cough, not the internet). It's because you are a source of knowledge. You can't be in the middle of selling an engagement ring to someone when you realize, "Oh, sorry. You wanted platinum? Damn. This only comes in gold. My bad. Will your fiancée love gold?" Know what you are talking about. Show your value as a salesperson. And it's *easy*. Just do the work. Memorize the info. Ready, set, GO!

#5: Your Approach Is Stale

Complacency is the real death of a salesman. Take a very long, hard look at yourself. Are you mindlessly and robotically going through the same pitch? Are you connecting with every single customer who walks in with the same tired line about how the cold weather sucks? Are you not feeling excited about going to work and potentially selling a ton of stuff? If any of that sounds familiar, you might need to shake up your approach. I understand what this feels like. Not too long ago I felt like Bill Murray in the movie *Groundhog Day*. My life felt like it was the same every day—wake up, exercise, go to an apartment, meeting, meeting, phone call, another apartment—and I felt stuck. Emilia came up with the perfect solution for my problem, and it turned out to be simple (and bonus, fun!). When a big listing came in, I decided to swap it with another team member for a smaller listing. It forced me into a situation where I faced different challenges and was exercising a different skill set. I ended up having a great time, and it was just what I needed to get excited about sales again. If you're feeling stuck, consider working with a different kind of ball for a while—this will help to shake up your approach. You'll be surprised by the difference this can make.

#6: You're Overly Focused on the Money

The day my credit card was declined at the grocery store was *the worst*. If someone had said to me, "Ryan, the reason you aren't selling anything is because you're too focused on the money," I would have punched them. This is the last advice anyone with money problems wants to hear—especially from someone who has money. I do know that if you're going into a sale with nothing else but money on your mind, it can impact the deal. For example, instead of saving a deal by cutting commission to bridge the gap, your ego gets in the way because you're focused on the full commission—and then the deal dies and you made zero anyway. Or, you push a deal too hard because you just want to wrap it up and get paid, and then you're a car salesman and your client fires you and buys the same product with someone else.

Worrying about bills, rent, the mortgage, and food is incredibly stressful, and I never want to feel that way again. It's hard, but make every attempt to shift your focus from financial issues back to the deal. Focusing on the deal and not the money can get you back on track. At the 2010 Winter Olympics, Shaun White had the gold medal in snowboarding in the bag before he even hit his final run down the half-pipe. He could have just coasted it. Instead, he crushed it. Why? Because he rode like he'd already won. Technically he *had* already won, but the psychology of going into a pitch with the confidence that you've already won can produce amazing results.

Ultimately, we've all been there. We've dropped balls, lost sales, and had deals fall apart. It's the worst! But I always try to remind myself that this is par for the course. If Derek Jeter struck out during a game, he wouldn't toss the bat aside and scream, "I obviously suck! I quit," and go off to live a quiet life as a peanut farmer. That would be crazy. Focusing on that one deal gone wrong (or, okay, a few dropped balls) can infect your entire career and your whole life—like a cancer! Don't let it. Deals will always die, and that's okay—especially if you have multiple balls in the air. I had a big deal die last week. It sucked, but I didn't spend the day on the sofa eating Lucky Charms out of the box and watching reruns of *Saved by the Bell*. How is that helpful? Yesterday I made a huge sale. I didn't put down the phone after the deal was done and say to my team, "Well that's awesome. See you guys later! I'm going to take the afternoon off to watch *Narcos* on Netflix and eat nachos." I keep at it, tend to my other balls, and focus on the bigger picture (the one where I have the best month of sales ever).

Serhant Secret #21

When I don't get a piece of business, I want to know why. *Why* not me!? I'm awesome! The truth is, there are some factors you just can't control, and you shouldn't waste energy obsessing over them. Move on and go for other balls.

IF YOU EVER FEEL LIKE QUITTING, PLEASE READ THIS FIRST!

Sales is the hardest job there is. In some jobs, there's no safety net like a regular paycheck or a boss to direct you. There's no guarantee that a big sale will actually go through. Salespeople have the most amazing highs, but the lows are painful. Sales can be exhausting, frustrating, and disappointing at times. But if you find yourself standing on the precipice, please consider the following first:

Have You Set the Bar Way Too High?

Lots of people fail at sales because they have insane expectations. I'm all for encouraging big goals, but make sure you're making reasonable goals. Don't think you're failing because you've raised the bar too high for yourself. Recalibrate your goals, if necessary. If you're just learning to ski, you don't go down the highest mountain first, because you'll probably die. You start with the bunny hill, then take on the medium hill, and when you've nailed those, you can think about hitting the black diamond—once you've gained the skills and experience to ski down it without breaking your neck. And remember, if you're at the bottom? Fine! Up is the only available direction. (Remember, I'm the guy who made just over $9,000 my first year in sales only ten years ago.)

Is Inaction Stressing You Out? Remember Your WHY.

Not taking action can make you feel terrible. If you're in a sales slump, you can't wake up thinking, *Oh, I can feel it. Today's the day everything will turn around.* That is very wishful thinking—the only thing that can change your situation is you. Do you love the product you're selling? Your Why is like a powerful vitamin pill—it provides that extra boost of energy you need to take control and move forward.

When Is the Last Time You Gave Yourself a Reward?

You've had a bunch of deals die? You're in a slump? It may sound counterintuitive, but I think the best thing to do right now is to reward yourself. I'm not saying you should necessarily buy a luxury car, but reward yourself with something that will boost your spirits and your confidence. Buy a new suit or handbag so you feel great at your next pitch meeting. It doesn't have to be something big—a crazy purple tie catches your eye? Get it, and know you look fantastic the next time you meet with a potential client. In 2014, I had a really slow month. So, I bought my first apartment. My budget was about $1.5 million, but I spent almost $4 million on a penthouse in West SoHo. It was the most terrifying thing I'd ever done in my life. But it catapulted my sales for the rest of the year because it set a new wall for me. I had bought it. Now I had to pay for it, or I was dead.

Serhant Secret #22

Remember that there is always an action you can take.
There is always something you can do, right now,
to change the outcome of your career.

There is always something you can do. Maybe it's focusing on different balls, changing up your pitch, or shifting your energy from the money back to the deal. Call up someone who didn't hire you and politely ask for feedback. Use that information to improve and refine your skills. Try something—anything! And in the end, where does it get you tomorrow if you quit today? Nowhere. Face your challenges head-on, and chances are you'll end up somewhere really amazing.

WHEN YOU FACE YOUR BIGGEST FAILURE EVERY DAY

The Brooklyn house on Ocean Parkway was incredible and the asking price was a whopping $14 million. In 2012, this was my biggest ball to date. It was the first listing I had at this price point, and I thought it would change my entire life. If I sold this, it would lead to more giant listings. I could hire more team members, move into a bigger apartment, and maybe lease a cool car! It would be a massive commission check and a huge step forward in my career. The house was in the Syrian Sephardic community in Sheepshead Bay, Brooklyn. It was 10,000 square feet with five bedrooms. The dining room table was so long you could have all of Brooklyn over for Shabbos dinner. Easily. The three chandeliers that sparkled above it were $300,000 apiece. The house had dome skylights with motorized shades, an elevator, and special heated sidewalks to melt any snow that dared land there. I put so much time, money, and effort into selling this house. And a year went by without getting an offer. Not a single one. For a year, I spent most of my time and energy on one very Big Ball. I was hyper-focused. I wasn't looking at the big picture or thinking about what would happen if that giant $14 million ball fell flat (which it did). I still love the challenge of selling something big, but that experience taught me how important it is to play with balls of all different shapes and sizes. I confront this failure every single day. I have a nostalgia wall in my office. I've framed a lot of articles about myself and my business that I'm proud of—big deals and awards we've won. But right in the middle of it all is an article that reminds me about my biggest failure ever. The headline in the *New York Daily News* reads: "$14 million! INSIDE Brooklyn's most expensive home." The article is all about that crazy house, and at the bottom is my smug, smiling, oblivious face. I framed it and hung it in my office as a reminder that no matter how much success I have, I will always fail, but I will fail smarter. I won't spend as much energy on one ball as I did with that house in 2012. I will be relentless in my efforts to get as many balls up as possible. Now I know full well that there's likely more failure to come, because the only way to avoid failure altogether is to do nothing at all—and that's just not an option.

THE SERHANT WAY

Balls will always fall. That's okay—sometimes there's nothing you can do. But incorporate these simple techniques into your sales practice to maximize your chances of keeping them up in the air.

Negotiating Tactics to Help Keep Your Ball in Play

- Bridge the gap.
- Play the fears.

If you're dropping a lot of balls, you need to do a self-check. Are any of the following an issue?

Common Reasons Balls Get Dropped

1. Failure to communicate.
2. You're replying, not responding.
3. You've set unrealistic expectations.
4. You don't know your shit.
5. Your approach is stale.
6. You're overly focused on the money.

Just don't quit. But in case you are thinking about it (but don't) . . .

When You Feel Like Quitting, Ask Yourself:

- Are you setting reasonable expectations?
- Is inaction stressing you out? Remember your Why.
- When is the last time you gave yourself a reward?

PRACTICE YOUR CRAFT

It's human nature (usually) to want to reply instantly when someone speaks to you. But in sales, how you respond (note I said *respond*, not *reply*!) to a customer can make the difference between closing a deal or losing a customer. It takes practice to do this. It requires you to fight your natural urge to talk. If this is a problem you struggle with, here are two exercises that can help you.

YOU SAY NOTHING EXERCISES

1. Just seriously say *nothing* for 20 minutes. Stay silent. Do you have any idea how difficult this is? I mean, I've never done it myself, but I imagine it would be really hard. Joking aside, this exercise can really help you think before you speak so that you can respond to clients in a thoughtful manner.
2. Sell something silently. Try selling anything—your car, your dog, your husband—to a friend. You can only use facial expressions and hand gestures to express why this purchase should be made. It's hard!

CHAPTER 10

Do It Right NOW

The letters read "Heaven's Gate" in ornate gold letters.* The sign rested on top of the most imposing, elaborate wrought-iron gate. To my 13-year-old eyes, it looked like the gate loomed all the way up into the sky. I can't even imagine what my 10-year-old brother was thinking. The gate was like something out of a gothic horror movie—it was completely overgrown with vines. In the four years we had lived in Topsfield, Massachusetts, we had never once seen the gate open—we had never seen anyone enter or leave. My little brother and I loved to ride past the big gate on our bikes, at the end of John's Lane. We'd always stop for a few minutes, making up stories about what was up there. Was it a scary old witch who hadn't left the house in decades? Did a mad scientist have a laboratory in a big mansion up there? Or maybe—as my brother and I both secretly hoped—it was Batman's house.

We were riding our bikes around on a summer day when curiosity got the better of us. We wanted to finally know—what was really up there? It turns out we were able to push the

---

* No connection to the extraterrestrial-obsessed cult of the same name that committed mass suicide in matching Nikes.

gate open just enough to slide ourselves through. We couldn't believe we were *inside* the gate. We walked up a steep, winding driveway with the most lush foliage and flowers flanking each side. About five minutes later we saw something that we couldn't believe—another gate. This one was smaller, but equally as ornate. We were getting excited. Only a truly amazing person would have a driveway and a gate like this. We were getting our hopes up. Could Batman really be our next-door neighbor? Oh my God. We passed through the second gate and continued walking up the long, curvy driveway—and in about another five minutes of walking we encountered yet another gate. What?! This house was obviously going to look like a castle. Would there be a moat? A suit of armor? The foliage got deeper. There were wild patches of roses that had grown like crazy. We passed a fountain that looked like something from a fairy tale—a creepy fairy tale, because it was full of weeds and the water looked green and it smelled. When we finally got to the top of the hill, we stopped. Right in front of us, where we expected the world's most marvelous house to be, was…nothing. We walked closer, not really believing this two-mile-long driveway with its rolling fields of roses and *three* gates could lead to just nothing. What we found was a massive hole, filled with cement. The largest concrete slab you could imagine—it was the foundation of a house that had never been built. We were disappointed, to say the least. Why would anyone build such a crazy entrance and plant all this stuff, and never build the house? We walked back down, got on our bikes, and went home to play video games.

I told my dad what we had found, and after a few hours of being punished for breaking and entering, he agreed to help us figure out what had happened. Why wasn't the house built? Was the owner kidnapped? Did they die just thinking about all that yard work? Was he a spy who had to flee before the house could be finished? We found our answer. It turns out that whoever owned the property was planning to build his dream mansion. He started with the gate, and he spared no expense. He spent a fortune on landscaping—flowers, bushes, and trees, and then the other gates. He shipped in gravel for the driveway from Italy, and olive trees from Greece. The entranceway to this house was going to send a message that the house you were about to enter was the Best House Ever. And what he had built was beautiful, but unfortunately, he had spent so much money on those details that there was nothing left. He ran out of money. He couldn't afford to build the actual house, and the bank eventually repossessed the property. All that money, time, and effort spent on a fence, and no house to show for it. I couldn't help but wonder—what would have happened if he had built the house first? To add insult to injury, my dad told me *Heaven's Gate* was also the name of a 1980s movie that was infamous as being the biggest box-office bomb of all time.

I remember how wildly disappointed 13-year-old Ryan was by that big slab of concrete. I had been hoping to go back to school with stories about how I spent my summer drinking lemonade with my best friend Batman and hanging out in his pool. There was no way I could have known it then, but that adventure with my brother taught me two of the most important lessons of my life.

1. There is no obstacle too big for me to climb over.
2. Do the most important things first.

Those simple lessons have impacted how I've shaped my work ethic and grown my business. I've carefully prioritized what needs to happen for my business to thrive. A driveway to nowhere is just a dead-end road, but a beautiful house without a driveway is still a beautiful house. And, as salespeople, we are constantly faced with obstacles—there are fences we have to leap, shimmy, climb, and fight our way over nearly every day.

The last message I want to leave you with is this: Be deliberate about how you grow yourself as a brand, and as a businessperson. Don't have analysis paralysis and overthink everything—focus on what really matters and then take action. And also, there's no fence big enough to keep you from reaching your goals. Obstacles are just fences, and there are a million ways to climb over them. They're not walls—walls are impenetrable. You run away from walls. Broke and afraid? That's a wall—get as far from that as you can. Just bought something you can't afford? Shit. That's a wall. Get as far from that as you can (by working harder and earning more money to afford it).

I know what it feels like to think you won't make it over a fence. Sometimes getting to the other side feels nearly impossible and I don't think I have it in me. But eventually I find a new way and I realize, "I've just had the most amazing sales week ever. I'm so glad I forced myself to keep going and that I found my way to the other side."

Shooting *Sell It Like Serhant* and working with salespeople who sell all different kinds of products showed me that we all face our own unique obstacles—we all have our own fences to climb over. To be an incredibly successful salesperson, one who is juggling multiple balls and regularly closing, you always have to be prepared to reach—to do more, to do something different. There are countless kinds of fences of varying heights and widths—and some might be really treacherous, like those covered in barbed wire. Chances are there are some fences that all salespeople have encountered, and those are the ones I'm going to talk about here (including my biggest fence). But I'd love the chance to hear about your fences. If we work together, we can always find a way over them. Social media has made it easy for all of us to discuss this! Tweet me @ryanserhant, or connect with me on Facebook or Instagram, and tell me about your fence.

THERE IS NO OBSTACLE TOO BIG FOR YOU TO GET OVER

How Can I Make Myself Stand Out?

After my Sunday morning workout, I usually head to my office in SoHo. It's my happy time. It's quiet and peaceful, and I spend an hour or two getting organized and prepared for the week ahead. I check out my calendar and clean out my inbox. If you haven't responded to an email I've sent you, you'll be getting an email from me on Sunday saying, "Hey, why haven't you responded to my email?!" Nothing gets past me. Sunday is also my cheat day, so I get to eat Doritos while I work.

But today is a little different. I'm meeting with my social media team to discuss a new venture. A few months ago, we decided that I should start a video blog. I realize that I'm a little late in the game when it comes to posting videos. There are nine-year-olds who have millions of subscribers to their YouTube channels dedicated to making slime. But about 11,000 apartments get sold in New York City each year, and there are about 30,000 licensed real estate agents. Most people would look at those numbers and think, "Wow, the odds are not good for making money as a real estate agent in New York City. Forget about it!" I prefer to look at it from another angle—I only did a small percentage of those 11,000 deals last year! How do I make more deals? Why isn't everyone using me? How do I let people know I'm out here and all I want to do is sell their apartment or help them find one to buy? I'm very fortunate that I'm out there on a national scale during the three months of the year that *Million Dollar Listing New York* airs. And now I get to be in the face of America for an extra two months out of the year thanks to *Sell It Like Serhant*. But what about all those other months? Sure, I'm very active on social media—I post on Instagram! I tweet! But that's not enough. I'm not just going to sit back and hope I get a call from some person who binge-watched *MDLNY* while they spent a week on the sofa recovering from strep throat. A vlog is a longer form of social media that gives me a chance to have some fun! I can be super personal and show crazy moments from my life that may or may not be real estate–focused. I want to give people a sense of what my weeks are like, and show them how hard I work. I know I have two shows on Bravo, but it's not enough for me. I'm not being snobby, and, believe me, I know when I'm an asshole. I'm just saying I still don't have market share. So, the vlog on my YouTube channel (YouTube.com/ryanserhant—go now!) is my new expansion of my brand. And if it doesn't work? It's not a big deal; no one will have been harmed during the making of my vlog. There's no good reason not to try it.

One of the biggest fences I have to face as a salesperson is finding fresh ways to distinguish myself in a never-ending sea of real estate brokers. The second I think I've left this fence behind for good, it crops up again, and I have to find a new way to hurl myself over to the other side. I always want to do more today than I did yesterday. I never want to look back at my career and think, "Oh, what if I had tried that!?" You know where you'll find the most wasted potential? The cemetery. As long as I'm alive I will do everything in my power to use every ounce of my potential and keep climbing over that fence.

DO MORE!

Offer a Unique Promotion

You can't wait for someone to toss a bunch of balls to you—you can't wait for business to just walk through your door. You need to give people a reason to show up. Autumn in New York is amazing! So, I decided to give out free pumpkins from my office in Tribeca. Fall is here, everyone! Rejoice! People who live in Tribeca can most definitely afford their own pumpkins, but that wasn't the point. This was just a fun way to let people know who we were and what kind of services we offer. It's not every day that you get a free pumpkin just walking down the streets of New York City—this was a simple way to make an impact. Talk to your boss and team members about what you can do. Samples? Buy one, get one free for a friend? There is always something you can offer to get people to remember you. Don't just make deals: create deals.

Use Your Sphere of Influence to Find a New Way to Distinguish Yourself

Amanda, who sold hot tubs, had children and she knew a lot of moms. And guess what? She figured out that hot tubs are awesome for families. It's like a mini-pool everyone can relax in! She started talking to other parents (at school drop-off, at the playground, anywhere!) about how much fun it is for the entire family to have a hot tub. Now, not only is Amanda "the one who sells luxurious hot tubs," she's also "the one who can find the perfect hot tub for your family." Think about who you know. Is there something unique about your sphere of influence? Perhaps you sell the best scented candles on earth, and you have lots of artists in your sphere of influence. Share with them that the delicate lavender scent of your candles promotes relaxation and therefore stimulates creativity! Think about what new connections you can make between your product and who you know.

I Don't Have Enough Money to Invest in My Career

Ten years ago, when I put on my Keeper hat, I realized that I could spend approximately $100 per paycheck to invest back into my business. So, I know exactly what it feels like to feel hindered by the lack of a marketing budget. Don't focus on what people who make a lot of money are spending. Stay within your comfort zone. Say you only have $10 a week to invest in yourself: That's enough for just about 50 stamps. Get printer paper and envelopes from work or school, and handwrite nice notes to prospects. Stamp and send. If you sent 50 letters per week, that would be 2,600 handwritten letters per year. You are *guaranteed* to get calls with that much outreach, and it only cost as much as two Starbucks lattes!

There is always a way to invest back into your career, even if you are just starting out. You just have to do it.

Social Media—It's Free

My social media platforms have been incredibly helpful when it comes to promoting my brand and my services, and I'm proud of how my audience has grown over the years. But I am not a social media expert—and there are probably a billion articles dedicated to the best way to maximize your social media presence. Social media is essentially your public résumé, so think about the image you want to project. The best thing about social media is that it's free—it costs you nothing to start posting beautiful Instagram pictures of the hand-knit organic sweaters you sell. Take advantage of the different platforms to grow your network and draw attention to the services you offer. For every two personal posts, post one photo or video for your business. People want to know what you can offer, but they want to know *you*, too. Remember what we talked about in chapter 3: People don't like to be sold, but they love shopping with (social media) friends.

Perfect Your F-3, the Follow-Back

I've been going to the same dentist for years. I've often thought about switching dentists, because it would be much more convenient for me to go to one that's closer to my office. Time is money! But my dentist is so thoughtful with his follow-back that I think he's probably going to be my dentist for life. About six weeks before I'm due for a cleaning, he sends a quick follow-up reminding me to schedule my appointment, and he includes jokes! I get his email, laugh at a tooth joke, and schedule my appointment. Get creative and personal with your follow-back. What can you do to keep yourself in the minds of your customers? Do you sell gardening supplies? Maybe you write the best-ever newsletter, sharing great tips for getting your yard ready for different seasons. Or maybe you pick up the phone every day and call each client who has a birthday on that day. That's the easiest form of follow-back there is, and I'll bet you're reading this and you don't do it! And P.S. follow-back and newsletters are also totally free!

Practice, Practice, Practice

As salespeople, our bodies and our voices are our tools. It's easy to underestimate how important our body language and the tone of our voice are when it comes to selling. When I was working with Mariel, who sells waxing services, I noticed right away that she tended to loom over her customers—she didn't get down on their level when she spoke to them. This is awkward and makes people uncomfortable (especially when you are trying to sell services that involve them being covered in hot wax). We worked together to find a way for her to interact with people more naturally. Jen, who sold skin care products, also needed to work on her body language. She tended to assume a posture that made her appear shy and closed off—she didn't exactly exude confidence. We worked on using mannerisms that made her appear more open and friendly. Amanda, who sold hot tubs, had the same monotone voice whether she was happy, sad, or sleeping. So, we worked with a voice coach to show her that her voice had range. When you use inflections, people respond to you better and listen to you more. If you can't afford a voice coach, stand in front of a mirror, make sure your posture and body language are strong and confident, and film yourself talking with your cell phone until it's not weird. Then show the clips to someone you trust and ask for honest feedback. And all the crazy exercises I've included throughout the book to make you a more awesome human? You should be doing those!

HOW DO I INCENTIVIZE MYSELF TO REACH MY GOALS?

Since my early days in the real estate business, I've always backed myself into a corner on purpose. Getting cast on *Million Dollar Listing New York*—when I was a very new broker—meant things were getting *real*. The show had confidence in my ability, and that was my first big shot to the head (metaphorically). I couldn't sit around in my apartment watching TV anymore unless I wanted the entire world to watch me fail, on television. I had no choice. I had to figure out how to be the best broker. Backing myself into a corner has pushed me to greater heights every year since. I bought an apartment that was four times my budget and the house Emilia and I are buying in Brooklyn will push me to work even harder (by the way, Mom and Dad, it will all work out fine, you don't have to worry—I swear!). So, set a goal the way we talked about in chapter 6. Tell yourself that if you hit your monthly goal, you can buy that thing you wanted. If you don't hit your goal, you can't have it.

Cut Out the Net

Eric, the guy with the big beard on *Sell It Like Serhant*, worked for a company that rented out apartments to kids just graduating from college. He spent four hours of his day commuting, which was bananas. I certainly understand that rent is expensive (I'll say it one more time, my credit card got declined at the grocery store), but making a deliberate choice to change your circumstances—backing yourself into a corner—can be the fire you need to get ahead. If you're living with your parents, consider moving out. If you face a long commute and you want to move closer to work, do it. If you're reluctant to fork out the money for full-time child care because you're not earning much yet, think about what you can achieve if you have everything you really need to succeed at your disposal. I don't want to tell you how to live your life—if you love where you live, that's awesome. My point is that acknowledging what actually might be holding you back from success, and dealing with it directly, can have a huge impact on your career. Cut out that safety net.

Plan a Trip

Where have you always wanted to go? For our first wedding anniversary, Emilia and I wanted to go back to Greece. But this time, instead of renting a villa and filling it with everyone we know and bringing along a TV crew, we were going to cruise the Greek islands in our own private yacht. I also had made big plans to eat ice cream during every day of this vacation. Our anniversary is the first week of July, and I marked it on my calendar in red. I've been doing this for years, and now the trips I take are just more extravagant. Every time I see the date of my vacation, (a) I get really excited; and (b) I feel incentivized to push myself harder—I want to make sure I'm earning this vacation. I'm not suggesting you do something outrageous like rent out the *QE2* or charter a private jet (but someday, yes, you should), but plan something that incentivizes you. Have something on the calendar that makes you want to work harder—and pushes you during those moments when it seems too hard to get to the other side of that fence.

Do the Important Things First

When I was ready to start building a team, I decided it made sense to look at what the über successful real estate brokers did. What did they all have in common? I noticed something right away—they had business partners. That's what I would do! I found a partner and we got to work. But what the Work looked like to me and what the Work looked like to him were different. To me, the Work (especially in the early stages of growing a team) was about making sure we had the business to support a team. To him, the Work was more about systems—having the internet set up and creating a good office space. I was out there making connections and chasing business, while he was in the office arranging the furniture. That partnership didn't work out, but it solidified a belief that I've held deep down since the day I discovered that Batman didn't live in the mansion next door. You must do the important things first. Had the Heaven's Gate guy started with the foundation instead of the big, fancy gates, his outcome would have been completely different.

Don't Wait for Perfection
to Become Amazing

I love perfection. My job involves looking at the most beautiful homes in New York City every day. I recently redecorated my SoHo office to make it an even more appealing place for people to work and it looks great. I even added a store with lots of clothes and things with my name all over them—always expanding the brand, you know! I also admit that I enjoy good suits and I think I've written about my shoe-buying excursions extensively in this book. But not too long ago I didn't even own a suit—I wore khakis and cowboy boots to showings, and I didn't let that stop me. In my first office I shared a desk over a burger restaurant on 49th Street. Don't get me wrong, appearances matter—especially in sales. But if you're focusing on creating the perfect gate, you'll never build the perfect house. Do not wait for everything to be perfect before you commit to being an amazing salesperson. You don't need the most beautiful business card to make a sale. Do the most important things first—building connections, creating business, finding more balls and learning how to keep them in the air. Look at the most successful people in the world—they don't even carry business cards or wear suits, but they carry themselves like Shaun White at the Olympics. Every day is a victory lap because they've already won. Now *you* should think the same way, and it will eventually happen. I promise.

When You Are Ready to Build a Bigger House

When most people set out to build a team, they do it backward. In my world, people plan to build the Best Brokerage in the

World, and they set up a fancy office and hire tons of people and assume that they will enjoy success due to their size alone. The truth is, there are teams of three and four real estate brokers who do billions of dollars in business each year (wait, that *is* a great business model). The amount of business you have should dictate the need for team members. You do not build the team and expect business to follow. You have to honestly answer the question "Am I selling enough to warrant a team?" before you start building one. If you're selling millions of pencils each year, yes, you need a team! If you're still selling a dozen pencils a month, keep at it and revisit the idea of a team when you have more balls in the air.

I now have a team of 60, and that is because I have built my business to a level where it can support a large team. When I started out, it was just me and Yolanda, who is now my director of operations. The two of us laid the foundation for our house. In my Finder role I made connections and sold real estate; as Keeper I made plans for the growth of the company—Yolanda was the best Doer ever. She took care of everything else. Thanks, Yolanda! Things were going well enough that we added an assistant, and eventually our house was ready for a couple of additions. We were now able to support a couple of brokers. We built our house first—the shelter that contains the heart of the business. And, sure, as everything started to grow and people began to take notice of us, we paid more attention to the landscaping, the driveway, and the gate. But we did the important things first.

Finding the Best Team Members:
Energy, Enthusiasm, Endurance, and "e"ducation

You're selling more pencils than you can personally handle in a day. Congratulations. You are ready to expand your house to fill it with team members. I'm still learning about the best ways to manage and support my team—their success is my success. But I've learned that I get my best team members, the people who are a good match for my goals and values, by following the Four E's. What I want in a team member might be different than what's right for you. But if you figure out what each of these areas looks like for you, and make a point of hiring people who fit the bill, you'll be giving yourself a great foundation for a winning team.

ENERGY

I have a lot of energy, and so does everyone on my team. Energy is infectious, and you either get a boost from the people around you or you get dragged down. I look for a person who is positive, confident, and has the kind of energy that is easy to connect to. Can we easily have a conversation? Is this someone I can see talking to and interacting with frequently? Energetic people also take initiative, and are relentless in getting what they want. That's a good team member.

ENTHUSIASM

Enthusiasm for sales and the product is a given. I look for team members who can inject excitement and passion into anything they are selling—whether it's a three-bedroom penthouse with views of Central Park or a small studio apartment that looks out onto a brick wall. Enthusiasm is the key to selling both. If I'm meeting a potential team member, I might put them on the spot and say, "Sell me this desk chair I'm sitting in, go!" I'll carefully observe how they respond. If I get an "Um, well, it's black and has four wheels," we might not be a match. If they say, "Oh, this chair is designed to maximize your best possible posture, resulting in greater energy and increased confidence! This chair will increase your sales!" we're onto something.

ENDURANCE

Sales is full of rejection. We all know this. As I've shared with you throughout this book, I've gone months without selling a single thing—and it sucked. I need team members who won't be fazed by the constant rejection, who have the grit to pick themselves up over and over again and get back out there. In sales, your endurance can be the magic sauce that sets you apart from everyone else. Endurance is the toughest trait to assess in a team member, but I have created a trick that works like a charm. I'm sharing it with you later in the chapter, so keep reading!

"e"DUCATION

Also known as the Little E, because it's honestly not as important.

If a potential team member is bursting with the right energy and enthusiasm—and I suspect they have the endurance to get through the worst of rejections relatively unscathed—education is considered a bonus. You already know the ins and outs of selling because you have years of experience? Awesome! I always consider education a bonus—you can teach people how your systems work; you can't easily teach someone to have enthusiasm, endurance, or the right energy.

SERHANT'S BIG BONUS SECRET

I actually debated whether or not to include this in the book. This is the trick I use to really tell if someone is right for my team. I was reluctant to share it because now everyone will know my secret and it will render my trick useless. My power is gone! But then I concluded that if you went to the trouble of buying the book and actually reading all the way to the end (thanks!), you deserve to be in on the secret. But don't tell anyone.

When I receive a nice follow-up email from a potential team member after we meet, I ignore it. On purpose. Anyone who has worked with me will tell you that I answer my emails within 12 hours. That's my thing. But not in the case of new hires—I totally ignore them. Why do I act this way? It's not to be a jerk, it's to weed out the people who don't really have the hunger. I want to work with people who aren't going to be deterred by my not answering—they will email me again, letting me know just how much they want to be part of my team. Those who do that are, quite simply, the right fit. My team member Jen interviewed with me just before I was going on vacation with Emilia to Greece. She had followed up with me after our meeting, as any good candidate would. Then I ignored her. A few days later she followed up again (now I'm getting interested), reiterating that she really wants to be on my team. I shoot off a quick response, saying, "It's been crazy, blah, blah, blah, filming, going out of town." I didn't commit to talking to her about any next steps about working for me—would she follow up again? She did. This email said something along the lines of, "I hope you're enjoying your vacation. I'd love to talk to you the Thursday or Friday after you return. Which works better for you?" Now I knew that when I got back I was going to meet someone who might be a good fit for my team. And I hired her!

WHAT DOES THE FUTURE YOU LOOK LIKE?

I've given sales all I've got, and it's been good to me. But as I write about this crazy ride I remember that it all started with an insecure kid who couldn't handle a single ball to save his life. He was the anti-salesman. If someone had told that kid, "Listen, it's going to get better. Someday you'll be the most successful real estate agent in New York City! You're going to star in a hit reality TV show, and you'll be so good at sales you'll get your own show called *Sell It Like Serhant*," Cryin' Ryan wouldn't have believed it in a million years. That kid would have just snuck into the kitchen for another contraband chocolate pudding, hoping his mother was asleep so he wouldn't get busted. My career in sales has taken me places I never imagined I'd go. Every time I work with a salesperson, I get excited about the possibilities opening up in front of them. Because I've been there, and sales has changed everything for me.

There are many people I admire, but I don't have a hero. I don't look up to anyone else but me. Everything I do is for Future

Ryan. And ideally Future Ryan has worked so hard and has been so successful that he can buy his own island and spend the rest of his days eating nothing but Oreos and ice cream. That would be awesome.

It would be even more awesome if he had changed the way the world views sales, especially real estate brokerage sales. That would be my Win. But until I turn the world of sales on its head and swap the island of Manhattan for the island of snack foods, I'm going to keep pushing myself to do more every single day. I have no interest in being the most improved player from fifth grade. If I'm not growing, I'm dying—and I'm definitely not ready to do that yet. I have a photograph of Old Man Ryan in my office that I made with an app. Everything I do is ultimately for that guy, Future Ryan.

What does the Future You look like? Are you drinking wine on your spectacular Tuscan estate and reminiscing about how whenever you faced a big fence, you'd remember your Why and find the energy to leap over? Is Future You taking your annual trip to Disney with all your grandkids, so grateful you did the Work, and that the effort it took to climb over every fence was so worth it? Can Future You even remember what it felt like to have your back against a wall? Does Future You remember all the challenges? Sales is a race, and it's a long one. Whether you've been running for years or you just heard the gun go off, you're still going to hit some major highs and lows. But no matter where you are on your course, just keep going. Don't stop. Your biggest sale, your best week, your most amazing year is still to come. Your Future You will thank you.

Ready, Set, GO!

THE SERHANT WAY

Never forget that fences are penetrable—they're not walls. There is always a way to get to the other side. A wall is something your back is up against. A fence is a mere obstacle.

There Is No Fence That Is Too Big for You to Get Over

Fence #1: How Do You Make Yourself Stand Out?
Solutions:

- Offer a unique promotion.
- Use your sphere of influence to distinguish yourself.

Fence #2: I Don't Have Enough Money to Invest in My Career.
Solutions:

- Social media—it's free.
- Perfect your F-3, the follow-back.
- Practice your craft.

Fence #3: How Do I Incentivize Myself to Reach My Goals?
Solutions:

- Cut out the net.
- Plan a trip.

Do the Important Things First

- Don't wait for perfection to become an amazing salesperson.
- The amount of business dictates the need for a team.
- Follow the Four E's: Energy, Enthusiasm, Endurance, and education (aka the Little E)

Acknowledgments

Thank you Paula Balzer for helping me create the world of *Sell It Like Serhant*. Without you, this book would be random deals, tied together by random thoughts. Thank you for turning my chaos into a playbook for salespeople around the world. And thank you for being my friend, and soundboard—we will laugh together about things that aren't funny for years to come.

To Emilia, my beautiful genius wife, for pushing me to write this book, even when I doubted myself every day. You're more than just my better half, you're the whole thing. You're my puffer love munchkin and I wake up every day for you.

To my parents, I love you, and can't begin to fathom what kind of scary, dark, disturbing place I would be in if it weren't for you. I know I was a little difficult growing up, but look! I wrote a book! It all worked out!

To Bob Dad, for teaching me the power of YES, to try everything, love art, and relish the passion in life.

To my editor, Krishan Trotman, for believing in a funny/smart business book. And to Mauro DiPreta, Michelle Aielli, and Michael Barrs for making this book a reality.

To Andy Cohen, Shari Levine, Frances Berwick, and everyone at Bravo for telling the world about me and believing in me for TWO shows!

To Jen Levy, for *Sell It Like Serhant*.

To Randy Barbato and Fenton Bailey at World of Wonder, and everyone at *Million Dollar Listing New York* and *Sell It Like Serhant* for letting me live this amazing life.

To Danielle King, my executive producer, for your guidance, support, direction, and love. You're one of my best friends, and all your instincts are right. That's why you make TV gold.

To my sister Misty, for teaching me to run a business. I love you.

To my brothers, Jack and Jim, and my sisters, Heather and Jill, for loving me unconditionally and keeping me grounded.

To Nana, I want to give you a big hug and kiss, but gently, because you're so old.

To Leonidas, Despina, Pickles (aka Mariefaye), and my Godfather Stratos, σας αγαπώ όλους.

To Jordan and Yolanda, for being relentless, and making us the hardest-working and most successful real estate team in the country.

To everyone at The Serhant Team for believing in me, my message, and making me look good every day.

To Natasha Bolouki, Marc Gerald, and Brandi Bowles, my agents at UTA, for helping to make this happen!

To my friends Caleb, Eric, Scott, Jason, James, and Chris—thank you for keeping me from becoming a social recluse.

To Fredrik, Steve, and Luis, and to the entire cast of the first season of *Sell It Like Serhant*, what a ride! You all informed more of this book than you know.

To all of my fans on social media, to everyone who watches my vlog on YouTube, and to everyone who watches *Million Dollar Listing New York* and *Sell It Like Serhant*—THANK YOU SO MUCH! I wouldn't be here without your support!!!